STORIES *of* AROOSTOOK

The Best of Echoes Magazine

Other Books by Islandport Press

Nine Mile Bridge
By Helen Hamlin

My Life in the Maine Woods
By Annette Jackson

The Cows Are Out!
By Trudy Chambers Price

Old Maine Woman
By Glenna Johnson Smith

Return of Old Maine Woman
By Glenna Johnson Smith

Wild! Weird! Wonderful! Maine
By Earl Brechlin

Evergreen
By John Holyoke

In Maine
By John N. Cole

Backtrack
By V. Paul Reynolds

A Life Lived Outdoors
By George Smith

Available at www.islandportpress.com

STORIES *of* AROOSTOOK

The Best of Echoes Magazine

Edited by Kathryn Olmstead

ISLANDPORT PRESS

ISLANDPORT PRESS

Islandport Press
P.O. Box 10
Yarmouth, Maine 04096
www.islandportpress.com
info@islandportpress.com

Print ISBN: 978-1-944762-97-1
ebook ISBN: 978-1-952143-10-6
LCCN: 2020932259

Dean L. Lunt, Publisher
Printed in the USA.

Cover photo by Brook Merrow of Stacey Mullen (Price), at age 14, picking potatoes in Leo Griffin's field in Mars Hill in 1987. The image appeared on the back cover of the first edition of *Echoes* and on the front cover of the 10th Anniversary issue in 1998. Stacey became a social worker and music director of the Mars Hill church where her husband, Cameron Price, is pastor. They raised four children and a total of 23 foster children.

All pen and ink line drawings by Gordon Hammond.

This anthology is dedicated to Glenna Johnson Smith,
a faithful contributor to and champion of Echoes—
an inspiration to writers of all ages who was proud
to be an Old County Woman.

Photo from *Echoes'* first cover. Photo by Gordon Hammond.

Table of Contents

(# indicates the Echoes *issue numbers)*

Editor's Note

Echoes: Rediscovering Community was published quarterly from 1988 to 2017 to celebrate the diverse cultures and natural beauty of northern Maine and adjacent Canada. Based in Aroostook County, Maine, the magazine focused on positive values rooted in the past with relevance for the present and the future. Its feature stories, essays, life stories, photos and poetry represented permanence in the midst of change and value in remembering our roots.

Echoes began as a brochure commissioned by the Association of Aroostook Chambers of Commerce and produced by Gordon Hammond using a magazine format. Because the publication looked like a magazine, people wanted to subscribe. Their interest inspired Gordon and me to collaborate to fulfill their expectations. We launched a successful campaign for charter subscribers, offering the brochure as the "Premiere Edition" free with every order for a one-year subscription.

Orders flowed in and *Echoes* took on a life of its own. The magazine was published, first from offices in Bridgewater and Westfield, and, after 1992, from an office in Caribou, Maine. At its peak it reached about 6,000 subscribers in every state and several countries and Canadian provinces. As the identity of the magazine evolved, community became the dominant theme of its content, inspiring the subtitle Rediscovering Community.

Echoes suggested that stories from rural places where roots are deep and traditions are strong can help us live in modern society. A calm, positive voice in a world looking for answers, the magazine was a portrait of home, whether home be a place or a time, a memory of the past or a vision of the future.

The idea for a collection of stories from *Echoes* existed long before the magazine ceased publication in 2017. In fact, we saved all the photo-offset plates and negatives from the early editions thinking if we maintained the same two- and three-column page design, we could produce books of stories from the magazine using the original plates. Computers made old processes obsolete, and an *Echoes* anthology remained a distant goal until Islandport Press expressed an interest in producing a "*Best of Echoes*" publication.

The task of deciding what stories to include seemed overwhelming. Islandport wanted one hundred stories from which to choose forty or fifty for the book. The hundreds of options published in 117 issues during the magazine's twenty-nine year life provided enough material for several books. Three people made the decision process both possible and enjoyable. Kristine Bondeson of Woodland, Cynthia Edgecomb of Limestone and Kenneth Hixon of Westmanland devoted hours and hours to reading past issues of *Echoes* and joining me to discuss which stories best fit the criteria requested by the publisher. Although we felt uncomfortable with labeling the selections "the best," we did *our* best to choose stories with a broad appeal that portray a sense of place and touch on the life and culture of Aroostook County.

Even though each selection is a stand-alone story, Islandport Press has assembled them into a cohesive sequence, one story flowing into the next, gently carrying the reader through the seasons of the year. I have read these stories many times in the last thirty-two years, but reading them as a single book, from beginning to end, heightens my appreciation of Aroostook County and of the writers, both native and from away, who call this place home.

If you like this collection of stories from *Echoes*, perhaps there will be a sequel.

—Kathryn Olmstead, Editor
Caribou, Maine
August 2020

Tell Me the Landscape

By Glenna Johnson Smith

For nearly seven decades the geography of Aroostook County has become a part of me. Now, after reading *Dakota: A Spiritual Geography*, by poet Kathleen Norris, I see more clearly my changes. Norris prefaces her work with the quotation by José Ortega y Gasset, "Tell me the landscape in which you live and I will tell you who you are."

I grew up on the coast of Maine in a cozy village with houses nestled together, protected by a low hill and ancient trees. Then, in 1941, as a new farm wife, I moved to The County, a land with massive, silent, empty spaces. Although I felt at home with the people I met, it took several years for me to be comfortable with the place.

First I learned to admire the big sky—the giant, inverted bowl that fits snugly over almost flat fields and gentle hills. Sometimes when I see a potato field that rolls right up to the sky, I believe that if I walked across that field I could see the whole world. On my early morning rides to the schoolhouse where I taught in those new years, I noticed the colors—cold pewter gray, bright Wedgwood blue, and sometimes a carnival glass riot of orange, gold, and red as the winter morning sun splashed the snow and the sky. As a child I stared at the bay; in Aroostook I stared at the sky and learned to love its moods.

It took me longer to accept the empty stretches. In fact, I didn't realize how much they were a part of me until years later when I was thinking of retiring and moving back to the coast. Yet always when I came home from a visit downstate, the wide vistas of fields welcomed me as I drove north of Houlton. I even imagined that there was more good air here—that breathing was easier. I take the time to watch and breathe—and I have learned to live in harmony with the dramatic changes of the seasons—the quick leap from snowbanks to potato planting, the soft greens of early spring, the miles of flower gardens when the potatoes blossom, the crisp fall when giant mechanized insects crawl over the brown earth.

I still have a love-fear relationship with winter. When the weatherman tells me it's twenty-below with a wind chill of minus-forty, I huddle close to the stove, my only problem being to stay warm. Or if I must start my creaking, cold car and keep an appointment or buy groceries, I see myself as a puny thing in a spluttering little metal box, trying to show off before God. I used to fear the days and nights when the swirling snows made an arctic wilderness of our farm, when the plows were conquered, when I couldn't leave home, and nobody else could come in. Yet at some point through the years I began to feel reborn in this isolation. As a captive in a cold, white world I could take a long look at my place and the people in it.

One night when I was a young wife, a group of us walked on the crusted snow from Easton to Easton Center. We sang and laughed as the moon made shadows on shining snow-mountains. For a few hours, we ordinary farm people and our ordinary routines ceased to exist.

Sometimes at the farm I'd go outdoors on a cold night and look at the stars. I'd listen to the silence and to a humming I couldn't define. I fancied it must be angels singing. I'd lie in the snow, spread my arms, and make an angel, just in case one might be looking down.

In some ways a blizzard is like the ocean of my childhood; both are fearsome and beautiful, and both jolt me to an awareness of my world. For many months winter dictates the rhythms of my life. Then in April I am delighted again to see the drifts shrink, to hang my washing outdoors on the line, to hunt for crocus blossoms and then fiddleheads, and to see young parents taking babies out in strollers— babies who are seeing their first springtime.

In Aroostook, it took me longest of all to love the winds. The stiff breezes back home on the coast rattled the chimney, blew the dry leaves down the street, and embarrassed us girls by flipping our skirts into the air. But they were generally tame winds, reined in by the tall trees and the hill. On the farm, though, the gale howled across barren fields and hit the buildings with such ferocity that it rattled the windows, tore at the shingles, and snapped at the foundations. Then it would turn tricky and be calm for a minute, only to gather such force that I would be sure the windows would break, the chimney would fall down, or the shed roof would fly away.

And that wasn't the worst of my fear. If I were alone in the house I'd huddle shivering by the fireplace, sure that something or someone was banging on the door, creaking up the cellar stairs, or dragging across the shed chamber. Finally one night, angry at my cowardice, I went outdoors without a lantern and walked all the way around the buildings. Although my heart was pounding, nothing jumped out of the shadows. I was alone with the flying clouds, the stars, and the wind. That night was the beginning of my conquering my fears, yet I still played the radio at top volume, trying to drown the mournful sounds. I can't remember exactly when the wind became my night music as I read and daydreamed, or when it became my earth mother, lulling me to sleep at bedtime, waking me softly in the morning.

It has been a slow process, me becoming Aroostook. Sometimes I wonder what my life would be in another place. Although I resist change, I believe I adapt fairly well to new situations when I have to. I could be content in Portland, Maine, or Portland, Oregon. Still, call me provincial, call me an old fogey—I hope I never find out who I'd be outside The County.

Harvest in Aroostook. Photo by Kathryn Olmstead.

Thirty Cents A Barrel

By Pamela Stoddard Taylor

"John Duncan going on time; Myron Gartley going on time; Willard Doyen going on time; Colie Guiggie going on time . . . all farmers going on time. It's going to be a beautiful day!" Wayne Knight's voice crackles from my clock radio at the ungodly hour of 5:30 a.m.

Having waited to the last possible moment, hopeful I'll hear, "It's raining and no one will be on the ground today," I reluctantly crawl out of my warm bed and begin to ready myself for another day of back-breaking work. First, long underwear, then T-shirt and jeans, flannel shirt and two pairs of socks, a sweatshirt, and old shoes. I add an old coat, two pairs of brown jersey gloves and a bandanna for my hair to complete the look. This is not for a fashion show, it's potato picking time in Aroostook County, Maine.

Having eaten a warm breakfast, I pick up the lunch my mother has made and a gallon milk jug filled with water that's frozen to bulging and head out into the darkness to wait for my ride to the field. There are no signs of life on my street. Even the paperboy has not begun his rounds.

The darkness of the cold September morning chills me before I even get to work. I've scarcely reached my section when I hear a tractor start up. The lags of the two-row digger screech over the gears as potatoes are dug from beneath the mounds of dead potato tops and hard ground to lay on the newly turned earth. There is no coffee to warm the blood before putting my hands and knees to work on the frosty earth. And it's only six thirty in the morning.

Potato picking can be monotonous. My picking style is to kneel down in the dirt with my basket beside me. (This is risky—I may soak my knees kneeling down onto an unseen rotten potato.) All the job requires of me is to fill the basket, lug it to a nearby barrel, dump the potatoes, and repeat until the barrel is full. Sometimes I get dirt in my eyes when I shake the potato tops too vigorously looking for additional potatoes.

Oh-oh! What's that oozing through the fingers of my glove? One of those hidden hazards—a rotten potato! "Oh well," I think, change to a dry glove and keep on picking. Because working conditions are so filthy, I never wear a watch or my contacts. (Vanity prevents me from wearing my glasses most of the time.) There is no time clock to watch and no break until lunch. A sense of time is developed from barrels picked, the position of the sun, or by creating a rudimentary sundial—finding a smoother place in the earth, checking for where east is, and placing a slender rock perpendicularly in the earth. *Voila*, the time.

Although potato picking can be monotonous, it is rarely boring. The two girls on either side of me and I have a contest to find the weirdest looking potato. I find one that looks like a Valentine heart, but Andrea has me beat with her potato that looks like Mickey Mouse. This morning I have my section all picked before the tractor chugs its way back up the field. This is unusual. A check of the sundial reveals that it is too early for lunch.

I listen for the tractor. No sound. A respite! The digger has broken down and will have to be driven back to the farm for repairs. The idle time is filled with water breaks—cold water comes from the once frozen jugs retrieved from several rows back, and bathroom breaks—taken in the woods if there are some nearby. If not, we push barrels together to create some semblance of privacy and stage our buddies around the perimeter for added security. It's not long before the steady putt-putt of the tractor can be heard as it resumes its seemingly endless progression up and down the field. We work steadily until lunch or the next breakdown, whichever comes first.

Lunch is a treasure to savor—it contains all the goodies I wouldn't normally get to eat at home—chips, soda, candy bars, and my favorite main course, Italian sandwiches. Lunchtime is a chance to rest, visit, and even play. Laying a barrel on its side across the rows I stand atop it and carefully maneuver the barrel down the row like a river driver moving logs. My friends show their appreciation for my talents by tossing rotten potatoes at me. It is truly "friendly fire."

The afternoon passes much like the morning. Barrel after barrel, row after row, we pick our way across the field, only to begin again in the next field. The older boys work on the back of the truck loading full barrels and tossing off empties. Sometimes Mike, the cute one, says "hi" or makes a personal remark to me and I blush like the teenager I am. From the cab of the truck I can hear the radio as it plays an appropriate choice—the latest Carpenters' hit, "We've Only Just Begun."

As the day ends, the pickers who are caught up help the tired, the slow, and the young finish their sections so we can all go home. Teamwork and camaraderie shine though the grime and the weariness. I gather up my discarded layers of clothing—my sweatshirt and coat— stuff my gloves in my back pocket, and trudge down the field toward the battered old farm truck that will take us home. Along the way I pick up my water jug and drain the remaining sips of now melted ice, saving the jug and cap for tomorrow. I picked thirty-seven barrels, a good day for me. I earn thirty cents a barrel and will put the money toward the purchase of new school clothes.

Potato picking is a six-day-a-week job. We don't work Sundays or those days that are too wet or rainy to dig. For approximately three weeks, or until the work is finally done, we bend our backs, pick potatoes by the handfuls and get them out of the ground as quickly as possible. Today, hand crews are rarely used to harvest potatoes. Schools in many Aroostook County towns continue to break for harvest recess, but crews work on harvesters and in potato houses.

I belong to a dying fraternity whose members learned at an early age the value of hard work, pride in doing a job well and the feeling that comes from making a contribution. We gained a real sense of community, even though the farmer and the crew that worked together for the harvest might not see one another again until the next harvest.

Countin' Tickets

By Jane Stanford

Grampy Russell tossed the contents of the wooden box onto the table—hundreds of dusty paper tickets with numbers on them. He reached into the box, his long arm almost disappearing, to pull out a few stuck in the crevices.

"There, that oughta keep you busy for a while," he said as he left with the box. "I'll bring in the red truck's later."

The red truck was only used when the newer blue and gray trucks were too busy hauling potatoes out of the field. That meant we had a big production day, which meant a lot more tickets to count. And I was old enough, now, to help.

Every flat-bodied truck had a box attached to the back of the cab, next to the hydraulic lift. Each box had a round hole in the lid where the truck workers dropped in tickets from every 165-pound barrel of potatoes filled by the pickers. Schools all over Aroostook County were closed for about three weeks so students and adults could harvest the potatoes.

Every picker in Dad's field received a wad of tickets with numbers printed on them—a different number for each worker. Pickers would stick one ticket into a groove on the rim of every barrel filled in their own sections in the field. And that's how we knew how many barrels of potatoes were picked.

In the kitchen, Mom grabbed a handful of tickets and formed three rows on the table, which was covered with old newspapers. She lined up the tickets in the order of their numbers. I did the same. Then I pulled out a "5" from my handful and looked at her pile. She already had several.

"That's Jean," Mom said. "She's havin' a good day."

Jean was the same age as my brother, Joe, who was five years older than me. Joe was working in the potato house where, as each storage bin filled up with potatoes, the men lifted more floorboards and moved the conveyors. The potato house crew also made sure only potatoes were stored, not rocks or dead tops from the potato plants that some kids put in their barrels to fill them up faster.

Mom's tickets made a snapping sound as she laid one, then two, then three or more on top of each other. Her hands seemed to fly as she sorted, knowing instinctively where number 10 went and where her pile of 22s were. My ticket piles kept falling on top of each other. I didn't leave enough space and kept finding different numbers in between the ones I already had.

After a couple of hours of sorting, Gramp came back with more tickets. He had them in a large cardboard box this time and dumped the contents onto the table, sending my ticket piles toppling over and the dust flying. I pushed the new tickets back into the mound in the middle and arranged the tickets I'd already sorted, making sure 11s weren't getting mixed up with 12s.

We finished just before supper. Mom had gone in the car to take her two loads of pickers back to their homes. Dad took more kids in the pickup truck with the caboose—a wooden cab with benches inside—on the back. Grammy Amy, who had come over to help, got out the bag of elastics.

"Number ones," she said.

I grabbed Mom's pile and mine. She put them together with hers and wrapped them with an elastic. We lined them up in numerical order inside a narrow, cardboard box. Then I folded the newspapers and put them away until supper was over.

The trucks hauled in later because the pickers had picked more barrels of potatoes than usual. They were picking faster because they could see that the big field was almost done and the faster they picked, the sooner they'd be finished. The weather was warm, the field was dry and the two-row digger didn't have any breakdowns.

Mom and Dad were both late getting back and supper didn't commence until six. Mom and I sat on the side next to the stove, Dad and Joe sat on either end and in back sat Gramp, Gram, and Albert Hallett. Albert used to work for Grampy, and then he worked for Dad. He had his own farm in New Brunswick, but every spring and fall he'd come over here to help.

After supper, Mom and Gram cleared the table. I unfolded the newspapers and Gramp dumped the rest of the tickets collected that day. In less than an hour we had them all sorted and put together with the others. Then we started counting.

I picked up one wad of tickets, rolled down the elastic a little, and flipped each ticket forward, using my index and middle fingers, until I had handled and counted them all. Mom told me to watch for any tickets with a different number and for tickets folded over that might be missed.

Finally, I took a pencil and wrote "32" on the top ticket and put them next to Gram to recount.

After she counted them, she said, "I make it 31."

Mom recounted them.

"Gram's right. It's 31."

An hour later, we had counted all the tickets at least twice to make sure our totals were correct. Dad came out of the other room where he had been watching TV and taking a nap.

"Would you mind getting my adding machine?" he asked.

I went into the little office next to the kitchen, opened the top right drawer of the roll-top desk and pulled out the Lightning Adding Machine. It was painted a metallic green and had seven round dials in a horizontal row across the front. Each dial looked like a minia-ture telephone dial and a brown stand held the machine in a slanted position. I found the metal pencil that went with the machine and handed everything to Dad.

"Number 37," Mom said.

She paused and said, "52," which was the number of barrels the picker with number 37 tickets had picked.

"Boys," Dad said, "he did good today."

He took his metal pen and placed the point in one of the dial holes and twirled it around just as you would if you put your finger in a telephone dial and twirled it around to get the number you wanted. Then he twirled the one next to it to record 52.

He kept adding more and more barrel totals onto the machine. The total figure showed up in the slots above the dials. At the end of the tabulations, the top number on the machine—1,625—was the grand total of barrels picked that day.

"That was the best day we've had yet," he said, pushing the machine back and folding his hands.

Mom wrote the number down in her spiral leather binder that listed, on lined pages, the pickers' names and ticket numbers, the totals they picked each day and the grand totals each day in barrels and hundredweight. A good day was around 1,200 barrels. At the end of each workweek, Mom multiplied the pickers' totals by 25 cents—the going rate for a barrel of potatoes in 1964—and Dad handed out the checks.

Mom put away her binder on top of the desk. I put the cardboard box of ticket bundles on the enclosed porch. The next morning the pickers would see if our totals were right or if they thought they might have picked more and the tickets had blown off their barrels or somehow went missing.

Gram, Gramp, and Albert had already left for the night. It was almost nine o'clock, past Dad's harvest bedtime. I heard his feet slowly ascend the creaking stairs. He'd be up before five. If he thought it was going to rain, he'd be up earlier to hear the forecast, see if it had rained already, and answer phone calls from workers wondering. He'd also call the radio station if he wasn't digging because the ground was too wet.

In 1964, some farmers had started using mechanical harvesters, but Dad said the machines bruised the potatoes more than hand crews and he wanted perfect potatoes. He wasn't planning on farming too many more years and if he invested in new equipment now, he wouldn't get his money's worth.

I couldn't imagine Dad and Mom not farming and life not continuing as it had. I didn't want anything to change, except me counting tickets faster and better, like the adults.

Harvest, 1961
By Linda R. Emery

The storm door slammed behind me as I ran down the back steps and across two neighboring yards. As I passed the first telephone pole, a soft whoosh overhead caught my attention. A snowy owl in full arctic white plumage lifted off, startled from its perch. The pickup truck waited at the corner, its headlights piercing the predawn darkness. I climbed in and found a seat in the covered, bench-lined back of the truck. The other kids were huddled together, somnolent and raggedy, looking like prisoners of the gulag on their way to the rock pile. My best friend, Liz, jumped in and crash-landed beside me as the truck lurched forward and made its way down the still sleeping street. We had both just started the sixth grade in mid-August and now, as was customary, school had been interrupted after the first few weeks for the harvest.

It was cold. There had been a freeze overnight and it felt like winter even though it was only mid-September. We checked our lunches—Liz's mother always sent enough cream-filled cupcakes for both of us—and we groaned over the same old, same old—bologna sandwiches and chips. Nothing good to trade today. We arrived at the potato field and found the digger idling. Because of the freeze, it would be a while before its blades would undermine the rows, exposing the new potatoes and sifting the dirt from the plant tops. So we sat on top of an overturned barrel, kicking against the staves to keep our feet from freezing, breathing out in frosty puffs in the still air. We looked out across the patchwork of fields and woods and could just make out Blue Bell Mountain across the Canadian border. I loved being able to see so far—all the way into another country.

The tractor slid into gear and we could hear the jingle of the chains as it began to sift its harvest above ground. We raced to the pile of Micmac baskets, picked out our favorites, and counted the numbered tickets that we were given to mark our barrels, which ensured that we received twenty-five cents for each one we filled. We stood at our designated sections of field, waiting for the digger to pass.

"Hi! Good morning!" We called to Jack, the tractor driver. We liked Jack and looked forward to each pass of the tractor, because he would have a new joke to tell us and it made us forget how much our backs hurt and how cold our hands were. He chugged along the row and disappeared over the rise, his red-and-black Mackinaw standing out against the cobalt sky.

We bent at the waist, shook the dead tops free and threw the potatoes between our legs into the basket, working quickly so that we did not fall behind. By the time the last heavy basketful was emptied into the barrel, we were a fair hike from our starting point. In the distance we could hear cheers coming from the pickers further up the field, a sure sign that the digger had broken down! This was great news, for it meant an unscheduled break that could last an hour or more.

As it began to warm up, we sat between the unturned rows with our backs against one row, legs draped over the other, cradled in the dark soil. It would be a good time for a snack and some giggly chatter about the very cute boy who was working on the potato truck that lifted our barrels.

The welcome break turned into an early lunch. The digger would be repaired soon after, so we knew we had better fill our stomachs. As I sood to retrieve my lunch, I heard a terrible familiar sound that could only mean one thing—the potato truck had run over my lunch box! I had forgotten that it was sitting next to one of the barrels I had filled earlier that morning. I ran down the field and my anger and embarrassment grew as I could hear the aforementioned cute boy's wicked laughter at the sorry condition of my lunch.

The pail was bent into a black "V" and Coke was fizzing out of one end. My sandwich was pancaked and mustard oozed through the Wonder Bread. It was peppered with field dirt which would have to be picked off or spit out in between bites. I knew the drill—I had been through this before. Mortified, I gathered what was left of my lunch and trundled back up the hill to slump down next to Liz, who was trying to be appropriately sympathetic, but was generally unsuccessful, nearly choking on her sandwich in laughter.

After lunch, it began to rain—a cold, drenching rain that came in driving, horizontal sheets from the west. We continued picking for a time, kneeling in the mud, dropping slippery potatoes, wet-gloved fingers getting colder by the minute. After what seemed like hours, the farmer came along with the picker truck, a sign they would quit for the day because it had just become too wet for digging the potatoes. On the ride home, I looked around the truck at the occupants. Two brothers were fighting over space and an older girl was complaining that when she blew her nose all that came out was mud because of all the dust she inhaled during her day. Liz elbowed one of the boys, as their scuffle spilled over into her territory.

As we hurtled along the dirt road, I leaned back and closed my eyes. It had been a long day. I could feel my face glowing with windburn and knew that my curly red hair must look like a fright wig—the sad result of a home perm and ten hours of steady Aroostook County wind. The truck rumbled onto our street and both of us jumped out of the back, waved to each other, and to the truck, and ran in opposite directions to our homes shouting, "I'll call you," and "See you tomorrow." I went in through the cellar entrance, stripped off my dirty clothes next to the washer, and put on the bathrobe left for me. I mumbled a passable greeting to my parents and headed for the bathtub to soak away the grime, sore muscles, and shivering dampness. Later, I slumped over the dinner table and ravenously devoured my reheated supper—"No potatoes please, Ma"—and then hobbled straight off to bed.

Snuggled deep under the covers, I put in the earpiece from the new transistor radio I had bought with the previous week's earnings. I had filled forty-eight one-hundred-pound potato barrels to buy that radio, and it was worth every sore muscle and every smelly, rotten potato I had kneeled in.

This was a great radio—if the radio waves bounced just right on a clear night I could listen to WKBW in Buffalo, New York. Tonight was one of those nights and I drifted into sleep listening to Wolfman Jack. The picker truck would be waiting at the corner much too soon, and I would do it all over again tomorrow and the next day and the day after that, until all the potatoes were in and another Aroostook County harvest had ended.

Things have changed in The County now and not so many children go into the fields to earn money for school clothes and radios. Someone said it was a violation of child labor laws. Perhaps it was, but now, in my 50s, I look back upon those days as halcyon. Those were the years that we, the children of Aroostook County, helped sustain the farm economy of northern Maine and learned a work ethic that would last our entire lives. They were the years that Liz and I were best friends, liked the same boys, had sleepovers and said we would be friends forever. Well, I can almost see forever from here and I haven't seen Liz for nearly 20 years. I wonder if she ever thinks of the times when we prayed for the digger to break down, for rain to come, for that cute boy to smile at us, and when we could see all the way to Canada.

The Pay-off for Picking
By Margaret Mueller Shore

I left my home in St. David, a hamlet just south of Madawaska, when I was eighteen, and have lived in a dozen places since. But no matter where I've lived for the next forty-odd years, come August, I get terribly homesick for Aroostook.

At the beginning of every August, I start thinking of the acres of potato fields with their delicate light lilac blossoms. Sometime between mid-August and early September, I give in to the yearning and drive to Aroostook. The drive is especially tiring from Bangor to Houlton, but I get revitalized when I enter Houlton and drive north on Route 1, amidst the roadside farms and endless rows of green potato plants. Invariably, when I drive through Presque Isle, I am filled with a joyful memory of shopping there every fall for my winter clothes.

The last Saturday of potato harvest was the *best* day of the year. The farmer stood in our kitchen door at seven in the morning with pay envelopes for each of the five children who had picked potatoes that fall. My mother who collected the envelopes, was instantly mobbed with questions like, "How much did I get?"

She handed an envelope to me and each of my two older sisters. Their envelopes contained $120, because they were older than me and were excellent pickers. They could pick one hundred barrels a day. (This might not sound that impressive, but since each barrel weighed 165 pounds, these teenage girls each picked 16,500 pounds or eight tons of potatoes in one day!) My two older sisters, earned more than enough cash to pay for their winter clothes and have a bit left over. My envelope had $72 in it—I was a twelve-year-old mediocre picker who averaged forty barrels a day (at 12 cents a barrel).

As soon as I saw the amount, I was already planning what I would buy. First priority was a winter jacket ($20-25), shoes and boots ($15-$20). I could also buy several dresses ($8-10 each) and other needed items.

Mom would help me decide what I needed most, and possibly I'd get a couple of hand-me-down dresses from my older sisters. Our two younger brothers earned even less, so Mom contributed to their envelopes so they could buy winter clothes.

It was 1963, the Saturday before school re-started, and my mother had been organizing all week for this trip. She had been through the cedar chest where we stored last winter's clothes, made an inventory of what could be reused and what would be needed for each child. She was armed with her list and the cash she thought might be needed, beyond our "picking" money.

By eight a.m. that morning, our youngest siblings were with a babysitter, while my mother and the five of us kids were in the maroon 1958 station wagon heading to Presque Isle. Part of the joy of that day was sitting in a car with clean clothes instead of our potato picking outfits that were always dirty and moist from the previous day's toil.

Although the three weeks of picking had seemed to stretch on endlessly, the thrill of a day of shopping in Presque Isle made the hard manual labor worthwhile. To us, Presque Isle was the "Shopping Mecca of the North." Madawaska had just a few clothing stores, and the disadvantage of the Sears Roebuck catalog was the inability to try on the dress or jacket before purchasing it by mail. Presque Isle had many stores where we could purchase most of our needed items in one day. To us, Presque Isle was the "big city." Until I was fifteen years old, it would be the farthest from home I would travel. As a kid, I visited Presque Isle twice a year—once by bus in the summer to attend the fair where I and my 4-H friends exhibited our sewing and gardening projects, and again in the fall for a post-harvest buying spree.

To understand what an event this buying spree was, you need to know that my mother was a nervous driver. She normally would not venture more than three miles from home, but Presque Isle was sixty miles! I'm not sure how she managed her nerves while driving five children in a station wagon over unfamiliar roads.

Nonetheless, shopping in Presque Isle was a big enough magnet to overcome her nerves. Armed with each child's envelopes and a list of their clothing needs, my mother would drive from St. David to Presque Isle with knuckles tightened over the steering wheel the entire way. We would arrive in Presque Isle at 10:30 a.m., shop at Zayre's and Grant's until noon and rendezvous at the counter café at Woolworth's. My two older sisters were allowed to shop on their own, and at lunch, my mother would review what they had purchased and check how much money each had left. Then she would prioritize their next purchases from her list.

Part of the fun was the sheer bustle on the streets and in the stores. It seemed like everyone within a sixty-mile radius was shopping in Presque Isle that day. Every parking space was filled, and every store clerk was run ragged trying to keep up with customer inquiries and requests. My mom was like a mother hen, corralling us together to prevent a straying child from getting lost in the store amid the hordes of harvest time buyers.

Lunch at Woolworth's was another joyful event of the day. We each ordered a hamburger and French fries with a five-cent Coke. My mother wouldn't let us order a milkshake because that was too expensive. Nevertheless, we were thrilled. We rarely ate out, in fact, for many years this was our only dining-out experience. I can remember the smell of onions and hamburgers frying on the grill, and the crispness of fresh-cut French fries (the frozen variety hadn't been invented yet.)

After lunch, my mother, accompanied by me and the two younger children, would stop into the S&H Green Stamp store to redeem her accumulated books of stamps for a needed household item. We had spent the entire previous evening pasting green stamps into books, which had turned our tongues a lime green. Then we had counted the books twice to be sure we had enough for the item listed in the catalog. So with full bellies and my mom's pocketbook full of Green Stamp books, we walked into the S&H store to get this year's item—a new steam iron. Then we continued to shop until three p.m. at which time we all met at the car to head home, the back of the car stuffed with children and all their new winter clothing.

My eldest sister, Marjorie, was always last to arrive because she insisted on going to Grant's to get a cone of roasted cashews for the ride home. She was very possessive of her cashews, but gave each of us one, then ate the rest of them at a rapid rate, before we could ask for seconds. I remember sitting in the back seat, hugging my bag of new clothes and dreaming about what I would wear on my first day back to school. I had decided on a new red corduroy jumper, a crisp white blouse, a matching sweater, beige tights (I was entering seventh grade and Mom insisted only high school students could wear nylons), a new white nylon slip, and a new pair of leather shoes that were bought a half-size too big so they would last for the next nine months. (My mom would have bought them two sizes too big if she thought I wouldn't trip in them and do bodily damage.)

Years later, after we had grown and left home, my mother refused to drive through Presque Isle. The city had grown, and by 1970, Main Street in Presque Isle had sections with two lanes and a traffic light and that was just too complicated for her. She was nervous that she'd be in the wrong lane, unable to change lanes, and either get lost or be honked at by other drivers. This presented a problem because the family planned to get together for Thanksgiving at my married sister's home in Houlton. The problem was solved when a friend of Mom's explained a second way to get to Houlton, by way of Route 1-A through Fort Fairfield, which had no traffic lights and no two-lane highways. Mom was immensely relieved, and from that time on, used the alternate route.

In the past few years, whenever I drive through Presque Isle, I always stop at the new mall to do a bit of shopping, but I can't re-create the excitement of my teen years. I miss the hustle and bustle of Main Street, the sidewalks filled with people carrying their bundles of winter clothes and a mob of cars with drivers trying to find the next closest parking space. It may have cost my mom some extra white hairs for the drive, and us kids all had bruised knees and sore arms from picking for the previous three weeks, but that one day of shopping in Presque Isle made it all worthwhile.

The Barrel Man
By Ron Laing

In the 1940s, 1950s and 1960s every farmer in Aroostook County knew who Tracy Day was. He was not just my grandfather, he was known as The Barrel Man.

In Aroostook County, where potato was king, people were accustomed to seeing grandfather's Chevrolet snub-nosed trucks traversing the country roads as they delivered new potato barrels to farms. A big sign on the truck's body read TRACY H. DAY & SONS— BARREL MAKERS.

This huge agricultural area, commonly called The County, is the largest American county east of the Mississippi River. Aroostook contains 6,829 square miles, making it bigger in size than Connecticut and Rhode Island combined. For years potatoes have been the mainstay of not only the farmers' lives, but also of the general population. If crop prices go down, the whole economy suffers.

At the time Grandfather was selling barrels there were no harvesters—everything was done by hand. Potatoes were picked up in baskets by men, women, and children. They hauled four or five baskets of potatoes to fill a 13-peck barrel, depending on the size of the basket and of the person who must lift it to an empty barrel to dump its contents. Farmers occasionally tried using bags, even boxes, at harvesttime, but they always proved more cumbersome to handle than barrels. Lightweight barrels seemed the perfect thing—Tracy Day of Westfield, Maine, sold the very best barrels made.

When I was a small boy I spent many hours traveling with my grandfather as he visited farmers throughout Aroostook, selling them barrels. Day after day we crisscrossed The County, talking to growers on their farms. We'd sometimes go into the field where they were working with tractors and equipment.

Tracy H. Day had a down-home Yankee style of selling, which was unique and effective, and this made folks like him. Farmers knew him as an honest man—one who would stand behind his product—and he had a good item they needed. My grandfather made a good living.

"We have the best barrel ever made—one that will way outlast any other," he'd tell them. "These won't fall apart in the field, either." Prospective buyers watched carefully as he showed them a downsized sample he carried around in the trunk of his Nash Ambassador.

On my trips with Grandfather, I got to know him really well. Lunchtimes with him were great, and they seemed different every day. If it was summer, or even late fall, we might stop at a general store where he'd buy a half-pound of cheese. I'd watch the storekeeper cut a slice of golden cheddar from a cheese-wheel, wrap it in brown butcher's paper and pass it over the counter to me.

"Gramp," a name I sometimes called Grandfather, would buy a box of crackers, a couple of apples, and two bottles of Moxie. Sometimes he'd get a can of sardines, too, something I didn't like, but he did. Before we left the store he'd bought candy for later, perhaps even cookies, and maybe Canada mints, too. (Perhaps I just figured how I got my sweet tooth.)

With our lunch in hand, we'd find a spot beside the St. John River, usually under a big elm tree, and enjoy our lunch. Sitting on the soft grass and leaning back on my elbow, I thought as I opened my Moxie, *This is the greatest fun a boy can ever have.*

The barrel business was only part of what Tracy Day did. He also owned and operated a potato farm in Westfield, planting at least two hundred acres each year. In addition to this crop, he raised acres of grain, hay, and green peas on his Egypt Road farm, and still more on other farmland he owned. My grandfather rarely worked in the fields; instead he hired others to manage and care for his crops. When I was riding with him while he sold barrels, little did I know that in a few years I'd be the one caring for these crops.

Grandfather also owned a lumber mill in Westfield. Later he added a small barrel-making mill, but soon discovered that with his higher labor rates he couldn't compete in cost per unit with the product he purchased from Canada. For the bulk of his barrel sales he continued contracting with longtime barrel-makers, G. Green & Sons, of Centerville, New Brunswick, Canada. It was a match made in heaven. Green & Sons agreed to make barrels using his specifications—then he'd sell "the best barrel money could buy" to American farmers.

The barrels were made from tongue-and-groove white cedar staves. Cedar was also used for the bottoms because it resisted rotting and was light in weight. The hoops (bands around the girth of the barrel that hold it together) were split white ash with the bark still on, which made the hoops last longer and not dry out. Native American basket makers often made hoops for the barrel industry since they had the skills and know-how. These workers understood that ash trees must be cut at the right time of year if the bark is to remain. Ash trees cut in the warmer months, such as May, June, July or August, will not hold the bark, therefore are not good for barrel hoops.

In the mid-1950s, Day's barrels became even stronger when he required coopers to put seven ash hoops on barrels made for him. Farmers liked this improvement because it increased the container's life, and they were willing to pay the added cost. Soon, only barrels with double hoops on both the top and bottom, as well as on the top-middle, were available from Day & Sons. Many of these barrels can still be found in barns throughout Aroostook.

With production orders in place and drivers on the payroll, Grandfather combed the farmlands visiting, joking with farmers and discussing world conditions, as well as local news—selling them barrels before leaving.

When telephone service was extended to Grandfather's farm on the Egypt Road in Westfield, his sales increased greatly. Then, right from his kitchen table, he was able to contact both repeat and new customers who lived miles away. Grandfather became a "telemarketer" long before that term existed. Nevertheless, he preferred visiting growers at their farms where he could talk with them face-to-face.

"Farmers appreciated this," he once told me. "They often have questions. Sometimes they even ask me to help evaluate their needs."

There were times I went with Grandpa and waited in the car while he talked business with a farmer. While I waited, I'd listen to the Boston Red Sox on the radio. My wait might be long and the game over before he returned, for he was never in a hurry. Once in a while I'd roll down the window so I could listen to his conversation with the farmer. They talked about everything except selling or buying barrels—which was the whole purpose of our visit.

"Takes you a long time to get to the point, Grandpa," I said when he returned.

"Think so, do ya?"

I didn't realize it then, but it was on these trips that he taught me a lot about the art of selling. Later, in high school, I took a course on salesmanship and found out a few details about selling for myself.

"First—you must sell yourself to the prospective buyer," the teacher said. "Make the customer like you and trust you."

Grandfather knew this without ever taking a course. In fact, he'd already taught this to me without either of us knowing it. In studying my textbook, I discovered my grandfather could have taught the class— he knew the rules of selling that were in my textbook.

When the visit finally ended I heard Grandfather say to the farmer, "So how many barrels can I send you?"

"Oh, I can probably use two hundred and fifty. How much are they this year?"

"Same as last year, $2.25."

"OK, two hundred and fifty will be good. You should stop by and see Boone Packard over on the State Road. The other day I heard him say he's got to get some new barrels, too."

"OK, we'll do that. Good to talk with you. Our truck will be here Friday."

There's no doubt about it—Grandfather really was a salesman, a real businessman, and yes—a Yankee Peddler, too.

Once, when I'd been waiting in the car for what seemed forever, I quizzed him when he finally came back as to how we did—and got a reply I wasn't expecting.

"We sold three hundred barrels, got two cows, a plow, and $200."

"I'll bet that's where much of the stuff around the farmyard probably came from. Right?" I asked.

He gave me a wink.

Helping Hands

By Jane Stanford

Cecil Emery glanced back over the digger. The twelve new workers looked strong enough and seemed pleasant. They'd do just fine, even if they were German prisoners. The rugged men, dressed in baggy trousers and trench coats, took up their places in the field. The horse-drawn, one-row digger squeaked as it rolled slowly past them. Shaped like a broad conveyor belt, it scooped Green Mountain potatoes to the surface.

The men remembered that their leader, Adolf Hitler, had promised they would march across the plains of the United States. "What he didn't tell us," one soldier told the *Fort Fairfield Review*, "was that we'd have to pick up potatoes on the way."

Cecil hoped the men could speak some English because he wanted to chat with them about their homes and what they thought about the war. Little did he realize that he would learn much more. Long before the 1944 harvest began, the Aroostook County Farm Bureau Labor Association had been busy recruiting badly needed workers to harvest an estimated sixty million barrels of potatoes. Most of the able-bodied local boys were fighting overseas. Those left behind, even counting women and children, were not enough hands to bring the potatoes into storage.

The year before, under the guidance of Smith C. McIntire of the Extension Service, Bahamians, Jamaicans, and summer workers from several states came by train to help with the harvest. New England Boy Scouts also answered the call for assistance. This year, the Extension Service had signed orders and contracts from six hundred farmers for 2,750 workers. In August, the service sent recruiters to Kentucky to sign up 2,500 laborers. In addition to the Southern workers, about 1,500 German prisoners of war were employed. The men lived at Houlton's Army Air Field.

Fred L. Lamoreau, manager of the Aroostook County Farm Bureau Labor Association, was the liaison between the government and the growers in getting the German labor. "These men may not pick as many potatoes as the experienced civilian, but they do a cleaner job. They pick 'em, not scoop 'em," he said.

"Attesting to the value of these former German soldiers are 135 farmers of Aroostook County, whose crops might have frozen in the ground without this unexpected assistance," the *Review* reported October 11, 1944. The prisoners worked a shorter day than civilians because of the travel time to and from the base camp at Houlton. They arose at three a.m., left camp at five-thirty and ate sandwiches and coffee in the fields at noon. They arrived back at camp at five-thirty in the afternoon to satisfy regulations that limited absences to twelve hours.

The prisoners picked potatoes and did other harvest chores in fields and warehouses in the Fort Fairfield-Presque Isle areas, west to Chapman and south to Sherman and New Limerick. They were paid on a "gang piecework" basis for picking and on an hourly basis for other work.

Each farmer kept a record of the total number of barrels picked by the group and submitted a report at the end of each day to the guard. Farmers filed separate reports for prisoners doing hourly labor indicating the number of hours each had worked. The men were paid 2.3 cents for every 165-pound barrel they filled. But the government collected the going rate of fifteen cents. "Prisoners are thus earning upwards of $30,000 a week for the United States Treasury," said the *Review*.

Prior to the potato harvest, the prisoners had picked a large part of the pea and string bean crops, which were "on the verge of being lost due to the manpower shortage," the *Review* stated. When the men finished harvesting potatoes, they moved to the forests of Maine and New Hampshire to cut pulpwood. In addition to the prisoners at Houlton, three hundred Germans lived in a temporary tent encampment on the State Road in Presque Isle, where they waved friendly greetings to curious passers-by.

It was to this encampment that Cecil and his father drove fourteen miles from Fort Fairfield daily to pick up their twelve workers and an army guard, one for every ten prisoners. Although they were to prevent prisoners from leaving the work site, guards were instructed not to shoot at them even if they attempted to escape, according to a "rumor" reported in Tom E. Rott's column in the *Review*. On one occasion the guard told Cecil he had forgotten his ammunition. But "the prisoners never found out," Cecil said. Or if they did, they did not try to flee.

The day the Emerys' family dog, a huge boxer, ate the prisoners' lunches, the guard let his charges eat in the Emery farmhouse. The dog had waited until the crew was in the field, then sneaked into the clean room of the barn where the sandwiches were kept and finished them off.

"It didn't faze him one bit," said Cecil. And Cecil's wife, Aletha, cooked up a hearty stew for the men, while keeping an eye out for her two small daughters. She nervously declined the guards' offer to volunteer some workers to help her wash the dishes. Aletha regularly supplemented the prisoners' lunches with apples, candy, and tea. Many farmers thought the rations of four small sandwiches containing a piece of meat and maybe some cheese were insufficient for their workers. Some farm wives cooked soup and sent out extra food that was easy to eat. In New Limerick, Owen C. Nightingale's mother-in-law cooked a stew for the Germans every day.

The fall of 1944 was a wet one and it was on rainy days that Cecil found opportunities to chat with his foreign workers. He would join them in a cozy room in the barn where they gathered around a stove to wait for the land to dry and to decipher newspapers for word of the war.

Cecil became acquainted with their personalities, their occupations, their war experiences and their aspirations. Most were in their thirties and had families back in Germany. They were bookkeepers, plumbers, and mechanics. Some of them had been wounded. They said they would never forget the bombs. The youngest in the group was a tall Czechoslovakian who acquired a reputation for making his co-workers laugh. One day Cecil looked up from his work to see the agile prisoner standing on a wooden barrel watching local girls picking in a neighbor's field. Once he had his crew's attention, he jumped down from the barrel and strutted along his picking section with his arm bent, escorting his imaginary girlfriend.

Cecil developed a lasting friendship with a prisoner named Herbert, who had some military rank. The son of a preacher, Herbert could speak and write more English than the others in the work crew. He had a ready smile and enjoyed conversations with his American boss. Cecil and Herbert exchanged addresses and corresponded for several years after the war. The Emerys sent care packages containing food items like coffee and cocoa, and in one letter Herbert requested enough cloth, lining, and buttons for a suit. His responses were warm and appreciative:

"Dear Cecil,

Can you imagine how great my joy was as I received two days ago again a care package sent By you? I think you never can. I did not expect one because I haven't been asking you for one. Now the greater was my surprise as I could receive again such a wonderful token of your kindness.

In the present state of our food situation here in Germany, which I am not able to describe in the right words, such a parcel is like a present from heaven. Maybe there are men who can never understand and judge the plight in which we are in. To be plain, it is terrible and if no help in a greater measure is provided for our people, the sequel will be a nation-wide disaster. I have but one wish, may the fate of my people soon be changed to a more favored direction.

There are many people like you in the United States who lend a helpful hand to many needy men in the whole of Europe. Millions of parcels have already found the way across the ocean to hungry stomachs. Millions of Europeans have warm feelings towards the American citizen.

I am one of them, because I know the purse of the average American is not always in a thriving state. That means he sacrifices oftentimes more than he should.

All the expenses you have on my half, put as I have told you to do in the last letter, on a bill, which I shall pay as soon as possible."

Herbert's last letter, received just after Easter in 1948, reflects the kind of understanding and bond between people as human beings that resulted when "enemies" met face-to-face in the fields of Aroostook County.

"We need badly help from outside. We can never exist without help. We have lost the war, sure, but I ask you, do you blame the average German for the last war? Look at the present situation in world politics and you perceive how foolish the guy is who blames the plain people for the war. But again, I don't want to tell you things like this.

"How was your last crop? Swell or bad? I hope you got a swell one. Above all, how are your wife and children? I hope they are doing well!"

Yours truly, Herbert"

Sweet Corn
By John Dombek

Nearly everybody canned garden vegetables during the Second World War. Gasoline was rationed by the government. So were sugar and meat. The only person who sold things people really wanted—like cigars and cigarettes and silk stockings—sold them out of a closet-like room in his dirty gas station up on the North Road. He was not liked, but he stayed in business.

On special Saturdays, the movie theater manager allowed free admission to the cowboy shows to all who contributed a piece of scrap metal to the war effort. He also gave free admission to disabled persons.

To Joe and me, war was some kind of game that caused people to band together to sell bonds or to sound wailing sirens at night alerting townsfolk to turn out all the lights and draw the curtains and shades while volunteers in white helmets with "Air Raid Warden" stenciled on them walked the neighborhood in search of light squeezing through cracks in the black defense. During the day when the siren sounded, the war brought drills to St. Mary's School. The sound froze us. We stopped what we were doing and stood at attention beside our desks. On signal from the nun, we either crouched under our desks or filed in quiet, orderly lines to the safety of the thick, cement walls of the school basement. Talking was not allowed until the siren that froze us sounded again and set us free.

The war brought stars to the windows of some homes, cloth stars sewn on cloth banners and hung for all to see and be reminded that another boy would not be coming home again to Houlton. And it brought German prisoners to the pea vine factory a few miles from our home.

Joe and I were curious. What did they look like? They must be monstrous, ugly and hateful, these enemies of freedom. We had seen distorted faces in cartoons of a Mussolini, a Hitler, and a Tojo. What must their soldiers look like? We followed the woods to the vinery, then crept across an open field on our hands and knees to get a closer look at these creatures with large black P.O.W. letters painted on their shirtbacks. They were not ugly. They were young men, like the young men in town. We crept closer and one spotted us . . . his blue eyes met ours and he smiled at us and waved. We noticed he had short blonde hair and that his smile was warm and we knew that war was a game.

Mom played the game in her kitchen. She filled row after row of clear glass jars with colorful vegetables. Orange sliced carrots, dark red beets, bright green snap beans, light red tomatoes, pickles, and relishes. All were stored in our cold closet in the basement. Mom worked all day near the wood-burning kitchen stove surrounded by kettles of steaming, boiling water. When the job was done, she'd stand back smiling to admire the neat rows of jars set to cool on the kitchen table.

"Aren't they beautiful, Bubs?

They were.

The Sunday our family had the ham was a celebration. We had finally earned enough coupons to allow the purchase of a scarcity—ham. All during the previous week we talked about the coming Sunday meal. Ham! We hadn't had any forever it seemed.

Mom cut thick slices and prepared it in a deep pan, drenched it in a sweet sauce, then carried it on a large platter, steaming hot and aromatic beyond our memories to our dining room table, set with her best silver and wedding dishes. Ham! Our reward for being soldiers on the home front. Ham! Thanks for our sacrifice. Ham! A family celebration made possible by a war.

When the war ended, the entire population of Houlton gathered in the town square to hug and yell and celebrate—all except Joe and me.

On the day the war ended, we took up our make-believe guns and put on our make-believe army uniforms and ran out into the backyard to begin the game again between the rows of sweet corn growing in our victory garden.

A Farmer's Wife
By Amy Morin

Mémère had ten children, and my mother was the baby. Seven of these children lived to grow up and have families of their own. Two died as babies, and one died at age eighteen. My mother said ten children was normal for most families in the St. John Valley, and that many families were even larger.

Her parents got up at four every day of the year. Mémère made her own soap out of lye (made by dripping water through the wood ashes) and fat. When she did the laundry she pulled out the washer, a big round tub with a wringer in the back and a handle that she'd push back and forth to agitate the clothes. She'd heat the water in a big tub on the wood stove, put the hot water in the washer, take a knife and scrape her soap into the water and stir it to soften the soap before she put the clothes in to wash. The clothes were always hung on the line outside to dry. In the winter they'd freeze stiff and would be brought back into the house and draped over the racks and furniture to dry overnight. Just about everything had to be ironed, and Mémère had six big flatirons with a wooden handle that could detach from the cold iron and reattach to the hot iron on the stove. She heated these on the wood stove, which had to be kept going all day long on ironing day—summer and winter.

Mémère baked forty-eight loaves of bread a week during the summer. She had a four-burner oil stove in the summer kitchen and a wood stove in the house. She would make eight loves of bread in the kitchen stove and four in the summer kitchen oven on Monday, Wednesday, Friday and again on Saturday to hold them over until Monday.

Pépère had two crews—one working on the "mountain" and one on the big island between Lille and Canada. Mémère had to get three lunches ready everyday—one for each crew and one for the family at home. She'd just finished the noon meal and it was time to get ready

34

Photo by Ron Laing.

for the next one, when the men would come in from the fields. This schedule was repeated every single day in the summer. Mémère would also take my mother and her sister Mana berrying on the mountain when the berries were in season. They would pick buckets and buckets of berries, and then they would make jams and jellies.

They also had a big garden, and they canned hundreds of quarts of vegetables to get the family through the winter. Every year at haying time, Mémère would pick a nice hot day and evening to take my mother and Mana up the mountain where Pépère was cutting hay. They would pick berries while the men worked, and then have a big picnic supper. When it was time to go to bed, Pépère would have made a big pile of hay, and Mémère would throw clean blankets on the hay and the four of them would sleep on that wonderful smelling fresh-mown hay under the stars. This is one of Mama's best childhood memories.

Mama never saw her mother or father sit idle. Every waking minute something was being accomplished. Many times during our conversations Mama said, "Oh, my land, the winters were long!" They were cold, too, as temperatures of forty and forty-five below were common.

"Our house was near the river and it was originally built to be a hotel," Mama said. "The houses weren't insulated, and what there was for storm windows was not much good. It took a lot of wood to heat that big house. My father had to go way up on the mountain to cut the trees and haul them home, saw and split them for our wood supply. Of course, we burned wood year round, not just in winter."

When they moved into this big house the year Mama turned five, none of the curtains from the old house fit the windows. So Mémère made all new curtains, and Pépère said to Mama, "Agatha, your mother is a funny woman. When people put windows in houses it is to let in light and air. But your mother sees a window and she has to put up three layers to cover it up—a shade, a sheer curtain, and a heavy drape."

Mémère ordered meat from a man from Keegan who delivered every week and took eggs, butter, and a quart of cream in exchange. There was no refrigeration in those days, but there was a brook in the back of the house with water that was ice cold. Pépère made a little well, with a cover that fit tight on the top, big enough to hold two ten-gallon creamers. When the meat man came, Mama's job was to scoop the cream from the top of the creamer with a soup ladle. That cream was so thick you could almost cut it.

In the spring, Mémère would buy two big blocks of maple sugar (each weighing approximately five pounds) from a man in Canada. She would use one and hide the other to use in July on ployes, oatmeal, and hot bread with butter. Mémère would also set milk aside in dishes and cover them. She told everyone, "Do not touch or move these, because you will spoil it." That milk would get very thick. Then she would take a knife and shave the maple sugar onto the top, and she and Pépère would eat it. That maple sugar mixture was Pépère's favorite treat!

One Sunday afternoon Mémère and Mana went to vespers and my mother stayed home with her father. He said, *"Quoi c'est que tu penses, Agathe? On va chercher le sucre d'érable que ta mere a caché? Je sais bien qu'y en un de caché quelque part."* (What do you think, Agatha? We'll hunt for the maple sugar that your mother hid. I just know that she has one hidden somewhere.) Well, they hunted everywhere in that house and never found Mémère's maple sugar hiding place. And sure enough, a month or so later out came the maple sugar.

A few years ago, Mama and her sister were talking about that and trying to figure out where in the world Mémère had hidden the maple sugar. They finally figured out that the only place Mama and Pépère had not looked was in the wooden blanket box on the third floor where the wool blankets were stored. So maybe the mystery was solved.

"Out near the garden there was a small orchard with cherry trees," Mama recalled. "Maman loved to have a picnic, so she had my father put a big table with benches all around out in those trees near the garden. He also put a couple of boards between two trees to make shelves to put things on. Almost every Sunday afternoon in the summer my brother Henry and his family would pack a lunch and walk over to Grandmère's and Grandpère's to have a picnic. Sometimes they came across the field and sometimes they came up the footpath between the trees. Maman would see them coming and she would make a lunch for us, too. Then we would join them at the picnic table. Maman always had her nice homemade bread and butter. Henry and his wife, Louise, would have homemade bread and butter in their lunch, too, but the kids all wanted Maman's. Louise was a wonderful cook, but I guess all children prefer the things that Grandmères make. It's the same today. Those are good memories."

I have always regretted that I never knew either of my Mémères. The talks I've had with my mother have given me a little insight into what her mother was like. She was a proud, hard-working, talented woman, who was ahead of her times in many ways. I'm thankful that my mother's memory is still sharp so she can pass on these stories and give me a little knowledge of the Mémère I never knew.

Under One Roof
By Jane Stanford

The connective farm, once common throughout New England, consisted of the big house, little house, back house, and barn where families stacked wood, stored crops, cared for livestock, and did numerous other farm chores without exposure to harsh weather. Specialized farms of today do not require different buildings for a variety of crops and animals. Early farms that remain standing remind the families who inhabited them of the bonds that tied them together, like the buildings of the farm.

It was late. Every few minutes we could hear the sharp cracking sounds of our century-old farmhouse as it tried to keep the cold from seeping in. When the temperature outside dropped below zero, we kids huddled beneath layers of wool afghans, quilts, and thermal blankets.

Dad, however, headed for the barn. When the thermometer hit the lowest mark—thirty below—we would hear the thump of his slippers as he headed down the stairs, through the lower rooms of the house and out the back kitchen door.

The cellars under the two connecting barns needed to be kept above freezing to preserve the potatoes until March when they were bagged for shipping. The barn furnace was located in the northwest end of the farthest cellar and Dad made sure it was fed enough coal.

We were glad our winter duties could be handled in the daytime. No matter how high the wind might pile the snow outside, we still performed our chores in relative comfort under the roof that connected the buildings of the farmstead.

We kept the chickens happy by melting the ice in their water pail with hot water at least three times a day. They also got warm potato skins or scraps of fat skimmed from a soup with their daily portion of corn kernels. The wild barn cats refused to inhabit the cozy stable, so we carried table scraps and milk up the ladder to their quarters in the frosty hay-mow.

We all took turns feeding and tending the animals and, at least twice a day, Dad would don his dusty barn coat and hat and travel from the kitchen, through the connecting back room, shed, barn and milk room to milk the cow. The stable door's black handle was white with frost but the air on the other side of the door was kept warm by the animals and Dad was greeted by their large, brown eyes each time he entered.

One weekend night, when we kids were up later than usual, we discovered the degree to which Dad took advantage of the protection of the connected buildings. As we sat at the kitchen table snacking, Dad came running down the stairs and flew past us, wearing his flannel nightshirt and slippers.

"The thermometer's way below the last mark and I can't tell what the temperature is," he panted, as he reached for his barn har. "I sure hope those spuds haven't frozen by now!" He grabbed his flashlight and bolted out the door, leaving his coat and scarf behind.

We couldn't believe it. The coldest night of the year and there was Dad, usually a practical type, jogging to the barn and climbing down that rickety ladder in his nightshirt. Had he been doing this all along? He returned ten minutes later, relieved that the potatoes were safe.

"I didn't have to do a thing, but I'll sleep a lot easier now."

But we weren't interested in the potatoes. We wanted to know why he dashed to the barn without a coat.

"Now don't go telling your mother on me," he said, his smile pushing up both of his rosy cheeks. "I'm in such a hurry to get there, I don't feel a thing. All I need is my hat to keep my bald head warm."

And, like Dad's hat, the roof connecting the buildings of our farm helped keep the warmth of the family inside, safe and strong, despite the storms outside.

Rural Aroostook Women
By Glenna Johnson Smith

I met them first in 1941 when I married Don Smith and moved to a potato farm in Aroostook County. I grew up in a downstate village of women who were good cooks and housekeepers, even during the Depression, yet they often seemed tired and discouraged. It was amazing to see Aroostook women who scrubbed and waxed every floor in their houses weekly, did their cooking from scratch and hand-scrubbed the families' clothes. They laughed so much I had to believe they were having fun no matter how hard they worked. I couldn't imagine women so strong, so healthy, so energetic.

There was Augusta Mahaney—known as Gustie. She and her husband Luman were kind to me in my early insecure years in Easton. They lived on a farm, but found time to be good citizens, participating in community activities and attending all school functions.

Gustie always looked stylish and beautiful, and I never heard her complain or saw her when she wasn't smiling. If they chaperoned senior prom, Luman and Gustie danced every dance. It was obvious they had a good time together no matter what they did. One night I watched her and wondered how she could be so sparkling. Maybe she had help at home, I thought. Surely, she had done nothing that day more difficult than painting her nails. Then she sat down near me and I listened to her conversation, which went something like this: "I got up earlier than usual this morning and got my housework done up because I knew Luman needed me in the potato house for most of the day."

How can she do all that and look so fresh and peppy? How can she shed that potato dirt so quickly and completely?

She was one of many superwomen. I remember Lydia Mullen who had a family of big, husky, fun-loving boys. This was before the days of clothes dryers and drip-dry fabrics. What a stack of work shirts, school and dress shirts she must have washed and ironed every week, and what a lot of cooking and dishwashing, as well as cleaning. Yet she always looked as if she were having a great time—at home or helping serve a church supper or town meeting dinner.

I recall a story she told me: One Sunday morning she left wood in the stove and a chicken in the oven, so it would be hot for dinner when she returned from church. However, the boys came home, smelled the chicken, decided they couldn't wait for dinner and ate the whole thing. Then they put the bones back together and returned them to the oven. How Lydia laughed when she told of finding the skeleton in her roasting pan. I don't know what the Mullen family had for dinner that day, but I'm sure it was plentiful and tasty.

Early on I saw an example of the kindness of these women I admired so much. A new young Cooperative Extension agent came to The County, eager to be helpful to the farm women who attended the meetings for socializing, as well as the chance for learning something new.

At her first meeting the new agent demonstrated how to make a simple casserole—it might have been a potato or corn scallop. She talked about its nutritional value, and about what to serve with it. She demonstrated in great detail the process of making it, using many unnecessary cooking dishes and many unnecessary tedious steps.

She didn't know that every woman there often made that casserole in half the time with a baby on one hip and an eye on the kids playing in the dooryard. Perhaps her husband asked her to drive to town to pick up a part for the tractor, or maybe she made trips to the garden for fresh vegetables for a salad, yet, no matter what, the meal was on the table at the right time and everything tasted great. But those women let none of their experience show when they thanked the agent for coming and praised her casserole. She was doing the best she could, bless her heart. She'd learn in time.

I don't recall that back then these Aroostook women went with their families on expensive vacations. If the Easton High School basketball team went to tournament they might go to Bangor, stay in a hotel, eat in restaurants and do a little shopping during the weekend.

At home they didn't eat out frequently. Several families might get together on a Saturday night, each woman bringing her specialty, which resulted in a great meal. Then they might play cards or sometimes charades, which caused great hilarity. An onlooker would have suspected they were all intoxicated. Actually, there was little or no drinking in the homes of farm families I knew, yet sometimes the men went on hunting trips and came home with funny and probably exaggerated tales of drinking escapades. Like the women, Aroostook men also laughed a lot and seemed to love what they were doing.

I am grateful that I experienced Aroostook in the 1940s and met so many women who became my heroes and role models. Although I tried to emulate them, I often goofed up.

Once, for instance, I made a cake, which I wanted to be impressive. It was a chocolate cake with a fluffy white boiled frosting. I placed it on a white platter, put a ribbon around it, and then added a wide row of flowers. It was gorgeous—it looked like a wide-brimmed hat with flower decorations.

Unfortunately, I didn't soak the pink, blue and white bachelor buttons, so when I served the cake, little ants traveled from the flowers up the white frosting. I got teased about that for a long time.

In later years, I've met younger Aroostook women—some of them daughters and granddaughters of my 1940s heroes—who have the strength, energy, and optimism of their forebears. Maybe it's something innate to the area. Maybe the magic in the soil that produces such great potatoes also produces great women.

Saturday Night on Main Street
By Dorothy Boone Kidney

According to the lyrics of an old popular song, Saturday night is the loneliest night in the week. But this was not the case in my childhood and teenage days in Presque Isle. Saturday night then was an exciting time because it was the night we all went "up to town" or "down town," depending on what section of town we lived in. The farmers, of course, went "to town." It was an experience to which we looked forward all week with eager anticipation.

The Saturday night outing was more than just a fast race around the supermarket with a grocery cart. There were no grocery carts and no big supermarkets. You stood with your weekly shopping list in hand at the counter of a grocery store while a white-jacketed clerk ran about the store filling your order.

Saturday night involved much more than just the housewifely task of shopping for groceries. Downtown Saturday night was "a social outing along Main Street!" To derive the most pleasure from this weekly social event, we all vied for choice parking places. This meant arriving on Main Street shortly after supper hoping to get one of the favorite spots. The Newberry-Woolworth-A&P-Marston's Candy Kitchen side of the street was best because more people shopped on that side. It was a vantage point for viewing passers-by.

Dad, tired of hearing groans of disappointment from members of his family when we arrived at five-thirty only to find all the choice spots taken, finally decided to park the car during the afternoon. So every Saturday afternoon, right after lunch, he parked the car on one of the three best parking spots, walked to work; and after work, walked home for supper. After our Saturday night baths, our family walked uptown to sit in the car.

We weren't alone in this odd way of "car parking." At the insistence of teenagers all over town, many parents parked the family car early in the afternoon and later the entire family walked to their "ringside section of Main Street" after eating suppers of baked beans and homemade yeast rolls. We engaged in Saturday night "car hopping" long before restaurant "table hopping" or vacation "island hopping" came into existence.

To engage in this exciting social activity, all you had to do was stroll up and down Main Street. Some people stayed in their cars; others strolled. Strollers stopped to converse with sitters. Sitters cooperatively rolled down their windows and the visiting began. Shortly after our family's arrival at our car, farmers would be standing beside our front seat and talking with Dad (who was a blacksmith); women would be grouped on the other side of the car talking with Mama. My sister Kay would be hanging over her back seat window giggling with girlfriends while I hung out the window on my side socializing with my friends. After a reasonable interval of being visited, you took your own turn at strolling along Main Street and becoming the visitor, stopping at cars parked along the curb.

Girl-boy romances sprang up along Main Street on Saturday night, thrived, blossomed and sometimes culminated in marriage—as in my case. My favorite parking spot was in front of the A&P where I could watch a young, handsome, white-jacketed clerk through the plate glass window as he raced about the aisles filling orders. ("Please, Mama, let me buy a few of the groceries tonight!") I attracted his attention on a Saturday night and later married him.

Of course, Saturday night visiting from car to car was better suited for balmy spring evenings when the car windows would be lowered. In winter, we had to content ourselves with taking turns at being warm spectators or walking Main Street fast (to keep warm) and being watched with interest by girlfriends and boyfriends seated in their cars. It was a sort of dress-up parade, a great time of waving, smiling, window shopping, visiting.

Dad often picked up business on Saturday night during the waving, greeting and car visiting. Although his blacksmith shop was in town, he carried tools in his car trunk and would go to the country to shoe horses. A farmer on Saturday night would greet him with, "Hello there, Frank! Great to see you! How about shoeing my horses at the farm next week?" So Saturday night socializing brought many benefits.

And sometime during the course of the evening, the shopping did get done. Mama emerged from the A&P just before the store closed, with Dad carrying three overflowing bags of groceries—the entire week's food supply often totaling not more than eight dollars. There'd always be three Old Nick candy bars apiece for Kay and me on the bottom of one of the bags—three candy bars in those days cost ten cents! And in one of the little bags would be a box of peanut brittle for Mama (her favorite candy).

Just before we drove home, Dad would go into Marston's Candy Kitchen and sometimes come out with a rare treat—four small Eskimo Pies wrapped in silver paper (ten cents apiece)—and he always bought the Sunday papers. The papers would be carefully divided at home—the news for Mama and Dad, the funnies for Kay and me.

One by one the lights along Main Street would go out. Lights would be extinguished in the drugstore with its wire-backed chairs and marble-topped tables, the handsome, tired clerk would snap off the lights at the A&P. Mr. Marston would straighten his magazines and turn off the store sign. Ah, wonderful Marston's—ice cream parlor and candy store combined—with its high-backed booths, ice cream soda and lemon Cokes—where you could duck in to get warm, where the high school crowd hung out—all a vital part of Saturday night along Main Street.

A few hours later, lights would go out all over town—the lights in the large houses on Hardy Hill, in medium-sized houses on Blake Street and in smaller houses on Chapman Street.

Finally a light would be turned off upstairs in the blue-and-white bedroom in the house on North Main Street where my sister Kay and I would drop off to sleep sharing the same bed in a happy tangle of funny papers and crumpled candy bar wrappers.

Learning Together
By Glenna Johnson Smith

Somewhere there might have been someone as scared as I was when I faced my first class, but I doubt it. I knew I wasn't a teacher and I suspected the students would know it soon.

In the summer of 1941, I had left my snug coastal village to become a farmer's wife and to live in an Aroostook farmhouse surrounded by vast empty spaces. I knew I had much to learn, and I looked forward to the long winter for the learning and adjusting. But I hadn't reckoned on the knock on my door in late summer.

The superintendent of schools for Fort Fairfield and Easton introduced himself, and said that he had several classrooms without teachers, and since I had a college degree he could get me certified. I assured him that I had no knowledge of how to teach grammar school, and besides I was busy where I was. He brushed away my protests, and asked if I would like the seventh- and-eighth grade room in town, or one of the rural schools.

My husband and I knew we could use the money (about thirty dollars a week), and I decided on the grammar school in town. I wanted to choose the one-room schoolhouse near the farm, but I was even more scared of keeping the right amount of wood in the old black iron stove than of being a teacher. I imagined that I would either burn the schoolhouse down or let the fire go out and freeze all the kids.

I asked the superintendent for plans and methods for teaching seventh- and-eighth grade subjects and he said none existed. "Just visit the room and look over the books," he said. And after that, when he visited to bring paper and supplies, I would deluge him with questions. He would pat me on the shoulder, say "You're doing just fine," and tell me how his racehorse was faring. So I learned along with the kids.

The old square building on the hill above Easton Village held the three high school rooms upstairs and two rooms downstairs—one for fifth and sixth grades, and one for seventh and eighth-grades. My room smelled of floor oil, dust, and mice. The books were dull and worn, and although I'd always loved school, I could find little of interest between those faded covers. However, if I read every night I could keep a day ahead of the kids in all subjects but eighth-grade arithmetic problems. They were impossible: "How tall is the tree if the shadow is cast in the river where the boat is going upstream at ten miles an hour? And when will the boat reach Albany?" They made no sense to me. Luckily my new husband was good at math, and he agreed to teach me enough each night to get me through the next day. The Lord help me if a pupil got interested and worked ahead in the book. The prevailing teacher technique was never to admit to a student that you didn't know an answer. One should say, "Look it up yourself and then you'll remember it." I felt that if the kids had any brains at all it would take them about two weeks to learn that I didn't know anything, so I decided to be honest with them. I would answer their questions with, "I don't know, but let's see if we can find out."

On that first terrifying day I saw before me a handful of girls—gentle, quiet Lucille, Helen, and Christine, the O'Blenes girls, others that I've forgotten—who were willing to work hard for the teacher. They reminded me of myself at their age; I liked them right away. But three-fourths of the seats were filled with boys—grinning, wriggling, loud ones. I didn't understand boys that age. I had no brothers, and I had feared most of the boys when I was in grammar school. But I tried to act as if I knew what I was doing, and blundered along. While I was meeting with one class, the members of the other were supposed to be doing assignments. But the brightest ones would finish their work and look for more interesting pursuits.

One day early in the year the seventh-grade boys planned an all-out war. They brought their peashooters to school, and came armed with pockets full of dried peas, beans, and corn. While I was busy with the eighth-grade lessons the missiles began to fly. To give the devils their due, they didn't aim at me or other students. Targets seemed to be points on a map on the wall, probably the enemy countries, for we all felt the horrors of the war. Anyway, by noon there were enough vegetables on the floor under the map to make a good-sized stew. Yet I hadn't been able to catch even one culprit. I said nothing because I had no idea how to deal with the situation.

At the end of the day I dismissed the eighth grade, and I told the seventh-graders that anyone who had not used a weapon could leave, too. I felt sure that the girls had not joined in the battle—all day I could sense their disgust at the boys. I added that if anyone left who had done some shooting, I would not be responsible for that person's safety on the playground next day. The girls filed out, and one boy rose to follow them. A low rumble from the other boys caused him to return to his seat, however.

My husband taught at the Aroostook Central Institute in Mars Hill. Because he did some coaching after school, I often worked in my classroom until five or after, until he picked me up. So I told the seventh-graders that they would remain until I left, and that they would write "I will not bring a peashooter to school again. Shooting peas can be dangerous." I gave each a stack of paper, and instructed them to practice their penmanship while they were at it. They got to work with no protest. I had learned early on that I could trust these kids to have a sense of honesty and fair play. Finally one boy said, "My arm aches from writing."

I said, "That's too bad, but think how much worse you would feel if you had accidentally hit someone with a pea. Keep writing."

My husband was especially late that night. The boys awaited him eagerly; however, a couple of them cleaned the boards and erasers before they left (this was a volunteer chore, not a duty), and they all gave me a friendly grin and said goodnight—tall Albert, blond Dick, the two Waynes, Pop, Alan, others.

Although they were an hour late for supper, I received no complaints from parents. "You punish him in school and I'll give him twice as much punishment at home," was the prevailing attitude. Alan's mother said that he came home so mad at himself that he broke his peashooter into little pieces, threw it on the floor, and stamped on it before he ate his supper. But I saw none of his anger. The son of the high school principal, Alan, had been taught to respect school and teachers, even such a one as I.

One thing I didn't like during my late, quiet afternoons in the room—the mice in the basement would come up and visit the big wicker wastebasket where we all threw scraps from our dinner kettles.

But there was one boy who daydreamed through his classes, and I often kept him after school to finish his work. He'd hurry through the lessons so he could kick the basket and catch mice as they ran out. I think basketmouse was his favorite game.

Red-headed George and tall Arnold, the eighth-grade boys who sat in the back row, were bright and quick with their studies. When they had nothing to do they would hide a magazine—often *The Reader's Digest*—inside their biggest books and read the jokes. I knew what they were up to when I saw their grins, for there was nothing to smile about in those old geography books. I was glad to have them reading magazines, but since the practice would have been frowned upon at the time, I didn't ever catch them in the act.

Each morning after the flag salute, Bible reading, and the Lord's Prayer, I read from a book for a half-hour or so. The kids enjoyed that, but after the vegetable episode I decided I'd better keep their hands busy while they listened. So I taught them to knit. Most of the girls could knit, and they helped teach the boys. Also, mamas and grammies, who donated the knitting needles and yarn scraps, did some instructing at night. Sometimes a student would drop a stitch, and then read to the class while I repaired the knitting.

We all had agreed to make squares of the same size, and I promised to sew them together into afghans to donate to the Red Cross for the war. As the students got interested in the project, they competed to see who could make the most squares. One day several of them declared that Wendell (called Pop) was cheating because his grandmother, Myra, finished his square every night and started another for him. I assured them that since we were making afghans for a good cause they should accept help whenever it was offered.

With a little shrinking of some and stretching of others, the squares went together surprisingly well, and we were all proud to see one of the afghans displayed in the bank building before it was sent off.

One day the superintendent dropped in during the knitting and reading time. He said he saw it, but he wasn't sure he would ever believe it. Perhaps right then he wished that he had taken the time to instruct me in more conventional teaching methods.

Although I tried to be conscientious about teaching the contents of the books, I was as glad as the kids were to take a break from the routine. One day an enormous white owl landed on the peak of Ralph White's barn roof. We all stood quietly at the windows and watched the beautiful, dignified creature until at last he spread his giant wings and flew away. Then we looked him up in the encyclopedia.

As the year went on, the students asked to do more unconventional things. We had baseball spelling matches, and we played word games. And at some point I developed the bad habit of stalling for time when they made a request so I could think about whether or not it was a good thing to do. I would say, "We'll see. It may depend upon how well your work is done, and on how you act." One day George and Arnold said they had prepared a skit, and I said they could go ahead with it. One of them was a perfect imitation of me and the other was a student. I can remember only the opening:

Student: Do you think the sun will come up tomorrow?

Teacher: It will depend on how you act.

It was a witty skit, and we all had a good laugh over it.

As the end of the school year approached, we planned eighth-grade graduation. The tradition was that we decorate the stage of the Grange Hall down in the village, and that students recite poems and speak pieces. But this class decided they'd like to write a play. Starting with the idea of George and Arnold's skit, they wrote a satire of schools, students and teachers. We had fun doing it, and the parents laughed when they watched it.

On the last day of school we had a little party, and I was unprepared for the gifts the students brought me—thoughtful household items chosen and wrapped by mothers who seemed to forgive me my lacks as a teacher. After the students left for the summer, I put my head down on the desk and cried. I knew then that I wanted to learn to be a good teacher, and yet I must have realized that no matter how many classes I might face in the future, none would live in my memory with the shine of this first one. I hated to part from those wonderful kids.

I've lost track of many of them, but some I've seen through the years. Paul, Perley, Wayne, and Earl were my colleagues in the Presque Isle school system. When I see Paul, I often remember that I told him he could never make it through high school because his handwriting was so careless. When he earned his master's degree from the University of Maine, I admitted to him that I was wrong. I'll always remember young Perley for reaching his right hand behind his left ear when he was searching for an answer. Wayne was a jolly boy, but a serious reader. Earl was a serious student, yet a strong, outdoor boy. Milford grew up to be a banker. I saw Helen and Christine become mothers and then grandmothers. Helen travels, paints, and sings in a choir. Christine is a social worker.

Marvin's granddaughter was in one of my recent classes in Presque Isle. She was incredulous when I told her I had taught her grandfather in school—she didn't think anybody could be that old. I taught many of these students later in Easton High School, after having stayed home a few years with my first child. I have outlived some of the 1941 seventh- and-eighth grade students. Arnold was killed in an accident soon after he graduated; George died of a stroke—a brilliant young lawyer, with a wife and four young children.

Yet in some treasured corner of my mind we are all still there in the dusty old room with the mouse-inhabited wastebasket, playing some good-natured pranks on each other, learning together that if teacher and students like and trust each other, sometimes good things will happen.

The Old Pump

By Harold and Candide Sedlik

In the late 1960s, my wife and I purchased her parents' farm situated in the scenic St. John Valley—Madawaska, Maine. The farm had been in the family for many generations and we were fortunate for the opportunity to perpetuate a tradition. One cool autumn morning several years later as we were cleaning our farm garage, I discovered an old rusted, cast-iron object. I asked my wife if she could identify it.

"Certainly, it was the hand-operated well pump used in the schoolhouse on our farm during the 1930s," she replied. Somewhat confused, I cautiously replied, "What schoolhouse?"

"The house my parents occupied," she answered with a grin. I was unaware that her family home had been a former schoolhouse, and questioned her statement. She sensed an explanation was necessary, and proceeded to give me a lesson in local history. During the early days, towns would lease or purchase land from local farmers for the purpose of constructing one-room schools to accommodate fifteen to twenty-five neighborhood children from primary through the eighth grades.

Due to the difficulty of travel and the severe northern New England winters, teachers frequently boarded with local families within their school district. Families that offered their hospitality were often reimbursed by the town in the form of a tax credit. The school on our farm, built by Carice Cote of Madawaska, was known as School No. 10. The land was donated by my wife's grandfather, Israel Daigle, to the Town of Madawaska with the stipulation the building be used only for educational purposes. In the event the school ceased to exist, the land would revert back to its owner. Other rural schools throughout northern Maine can be located on early U.S. Government Topographic Maps.

My wife attended School No. 10 as a child and recalls the old cast-iron pump located in the basement and mounted on a wooden platform over a well. The pump was used to supply drinking water and to fill a large storage tank mounted to the basement ceiling. Water was gravity-fed from the storage tank to the boys' and girls' lavatories, which were also located in the basement. Every morning the older boys refilled the storage tank with fresh water.

School on our farm was discontinued in the spring of 1938, and the neighborhood children were transferred to Saint Thomas School in Madawaska. The building was then used as an experimental school to teach the art of weaving. The program proved unsuccessful and was discontinued.

In 1946, the Town of Madawaska offered my wife's family an opportunity to purchase the former schoolhouse. Her parents accepted the town's generous offer and converted the building to their family home. The converted schoolhouse remained on the farm until my wife's parents retired in the early 1960s. Upon their retirement, they abandoned the farm and moved their home (former schoolhouse) to a lot close to the town. At that time her parents converted their home into a two-family residence, which is still in existence today.

When we acquired the farm, remnants of the schoolhouse foundation were visible and created an unsightly appearance and potential hazard. As a safety precaution, it was necessary to have the foundation cavity filled and landscaped. In the process we decided to preserve the old schoolhouse well by extending its steel casing to the surface. Several years later I discovered the vintage pump in the garage and my wife suggested we resurrect and mount it over the well.

It was in poor mechanical condition and lacked several major components. It would require an expensive overhaul to restore our school pump to operational status. As an alternative, I suggested perhaps we should consider painting the pump and mounting it on a wooden platform over the well as a nonfunctional ornament. It would make an interesting conversation piece. However, my wife convinced me it would be an excellent historic gesture to restore the school pump to its original operating condition.

The manufacturer's name was embossed on the pump housing—"Deming Pump—Salem, Ohio." The company still exists and produces pumps. When I sent a letter with a photograph of our pump to their customer service department, their reply was not encouraging. Due to limited market demands, they had discontinued manufacturing hand-operated pumps and converted their operation to more profitable electrical pumps. They also discontinued producing replacement parts for hand pumps. Still, we were determined our old pump would once again pump water as it had seventy-five years ago.

Several weeks later, a friend suggested I contact Lehman's of Kidron, Ohio. Lehman's is a large hardware store located in the heart of the Amish country that caters to the self-sufficient lifestyle of its local population. To expedite matters we decided to make a personal visit to their store. Our trip was enjoyable, traveling through the Amish countryside with its rolling hills, beautiful farms, and horse-drawn carriages. Arriving at the store, I showed the salesperson a photograph of our pump, which he immediately identified as a double-acting force pump. This type of pump has the ability to force water beyond the height of its spout. This was evident when it was used in the old schoolhouse. In contrast, the common lift pump is physically incapable of forcing water beyond the height of its spout. He also mentioned our pump was unique and, from the photograph, appeared to be in beautiful condition. His comment was pleasing and reassuring.

We purchased all the necessary replacement parts with detailed instructions and were eager for our return to Maine to mount the pump on its original site. With the instructions as a guide, the pump was assembled with minimum effort. It was then carefully mounted and secured on a wooden platform over the well. Despite the many disappointments, it was a beautiful sight and a historic moment to finally witness the flow of fresh clear water from our ancient pump.

The old-schoolhouse pump with cast-bronze plaque remains on our farm today as a permanent reminder of and lasting tribute to all the students and teachers who were active participants in an early American rural school system. The following inscription appears on the plaque:

SITE OF

SCHOOLHOUSE NO. 10

1929-1938

IN HONOR OF ALL STUDENTS AND TEACHERS WHO

WERE PART OF THIS SCHOOL AND ITS TRADITIONS

My First Day of School
By Dan Ennis

There had been warnings that something like this "going to school" was going to happen to me and my older brother. However, it being summertime, I did not heed the warning words. About three days before we were to be sent to school, I finally had to hear what both my mother and brother had tried to tell me.

Mom sat me and my brother down on our front porch and told us that on Monday we would be going to school. She pointed to a gray brick building that sat on a hill about a mile away from our house. Being new off the reserve community for only about a year, I had difficulty speaking, understanding and comprehending the English language and non-Indian concepts like a school or education. The first things I asked my mom was would she be there with us in that school, and she said "no." That was the beginning of my years of feelings of foreboding, of fear, of being alone. She said that it would just be me and my older brother, which made me feel a little less fearful—my big brother would be with me.

I asked my mother why we had to go to that school, and she said this is just how it is in white country—kids have to stop being taught by their parents and/or grandparents and go to a school to be taught by strangers.

I said that since neither my brother nor I could read or write English, and since we only spoke and understood Indian, we should not have to go to this school. But my mom said that there was no way around it—we had to go to school. So on the following Monday morning we were awakened by our mom and told to get ready to go to school. That's when I began having that feeling of despair, that sick feeling in the pit of my stomach that remained with me until I was about thirty-five.

Those negative and fearful feelings only increased and intensified the closer we got to the school. I didn't know what to do—cry, run, throw up, or just give up. That day was a blur of foreign and fast-talking people telling me things. I had absolutely no idea what they were saying to me. I remember thinking I'd have to stay real close to my big brother or else something terrible would happen to me, so I stayed as close to him as I could. He was a little island of refuge and safety, he kept me from disappearing inside myself. That is what my brother was to me for the rest of our days together. Somehow we made it through that first day, and I survived only because of my big brother. I give thanks every day that he was there for me and still is today.

The next morning my mom woke us up and said to get ready for school again. My whole body and spirit went ice cold. I thought to myself, I have to go there again? And I began to get sick to my stomach. My brother got dressed and went downstairs, but I could not move. After a while I managed to get out of bed, but I felt sick and numb all over. I must have sat down on the floor, because that is where my brother found me when he came up to see what I was doing—sitting on the floor completely dejected. That image of a young child sitting in deep despair and helplessness has haunted me off and on throughout my life. As I got older, the memory of that first day of school faded and whenever that image or vision came to me I did not understand it. I had forgotten who the child was and tried to put it out of my mind. With the help of ceremonies, I was able to understand the vision of the lost child and to remember that that child is me.

Since our grandson came to us six years ago as a gift from the Creator, I have again begun to experience that lost child vision, only with the face of our grandson, or is it our son? Looking back now, it seems ironic that our parents took our family away from the safety and security of our little island of refuge—Tobique—to protect us from racism, hatred, lack of employment opportunities and lack of economic opportunities. In the white community we moved to, we suffered all those things, and for us kids, it was a hundred times worse because we had to go to school.

Henderson School
By Gwen Haley Harmon

"Henderson School" is from a collection of stories Gwen Harmon wrote for her nieces and nephews to enrich their understanding of their ancestors and themselves. The anecdotes portray rural life in the 1920s and 1930s on the farm of Leo and Margaret (McGlinn) Haley. Descended from Irish immigrants who left Ireland to escape religious persecution, the Haleys settled in Woodland, Maine, "nine miles from town and on a crossroad," in Mrs. Haley's words, and had four children: Burnham, Leola, Gwen and Doris.

Mom always hurried to the kitchen window to watch us when we started out for our daily walk to Henderson School about a mile down the road. We came into view when we passed the corner of the house and disappeared when we ran down a small hill, following the road through the woods to the one-room school on the corner. We appeared once more when we climbed a short hill and emerged from the woods. When she was satisfied that her three children were all together and moving on, she could begin her daily chores.

We wore warm sheepskin jackets, hand-knitted woolen mittens, socks and scarves, tasseled wool hats and laced-to-the knee leather boots, each pair sporting a small jackknife in a slim case on the right boot with a flap snapped securely at the top. Heavy rubbers were worn over the leather boots.

My older brother, Burnham, carried his and Leola's sandwiches in a battered black lunch box with a heavy harness strap handle. I carried a little red rectangular box with double handles.

Burnham and Leola often had to stop and wait for me to catch up because my legs were not as long as theirs and my beloved boots with the rubbers pulled over them slowed me down. We were always in a hurry because we wanted to get to school early enough to have time to play with our friends outside before the bell called us in for school.

In the winter we could see the imprints of the heavy board of the huge rollers that flattened the snow on the roads. In the spring the road would be impassable at times when a small brook would team with croaks, plops and splashes when we passed and we could not resist stopping to dip flashing black polliwogs into screw-top jars or cans to take home and watch develop into frogs.

The distance from the top of the hill to the school was not great, but some mornings the road was filled with high drifts and the north wind chilled our cheeks and turned the tips of our ears white. When the pain was too great, we turned our backs to the north and inched our way backwards up and down the banks and drifts until the pine trees surrounding the school came into our peripheral vision. Then we would turn, bow our heads, hunch our shoulders and with short, stiff-legged strides, run to the outside door of the entry into the schoolroom.

On milder winter days, we greeted our friends in the schoolyard for games like Fox and Geese and King of the Mountain. The early-bird students packed down circuitous trails in the snow of the potato field next to the school where "the fox" chase "geese" until the school bell rang. Younger students pushed and shoved each other on the high banks of snow playing King of the Mountain, while older boys built snow forts, rolling small snowballs into huge ones to form the walls.

At 8:15 a.m. one lucky student got to ring the handbell that called the rest of us in from the schoolyard. Reluctantly leaving our games, we all attempted to jam through the door at the same time. The boys stopped beside their coat hooks just inside the door while the girls pushed through the bottleneck to their row of coat hooks just beyond. Smaller children were sent tumbling to the floor in the chaos that occurred not only in the morning but also after each recess and lunch break.

We hung our snowy coats and hats on the rows of hooks and proceeded to take off our rubbers, a real chore. Dad and Mom cautioned us not to push off the heel of one rubber with the toe of the other foot because such rough treatment could split the back of the rubber, not only letting in moisture, but also preventing the rubber from fitting tightly. Many a time we had to return to the snowbanks to search for a missing rubber embedded deep in the snow. Worse, if our rubbers were too loose, they were held on with a red Ball Brand canning jar rubber around the foot just in back of the toe joints—the ultimate embarrassment and a good reason for us to take off our rubbers carefully. As a primary grade student, I waited for my older sister, Leola, to tug my rubbers off while I clung to a coat hook with both hands so I wouldn't be dragged across the floor.

We shook the snow from our mittens and placed them on the floor in a row around the long cast-iron woodstove. A piece of asbestos covered with tin had been placed under the stove over the scarred, heavily oiled softwood floor. This prevented a fire from starting if the coals exploded or sparks flew out as three-foot pieces of dry wood were shoved in through the front stove door or dropped down through the lifted top.

During the eight years I attended the Henderson School, the five Grant boys were responsible for starting the fire on cold mornings. One or more of them would come down to the school early so, by the time the rest of us arrived, the sides of the stoves and several feet of the stovepipe rising from it were red hot. It didn't take long for our mittens to dry.

As school janitors, the Grant boys also were responsible for keeping the cooler filled with drinking water. As soon as outside wraps were removed, those wanting drinks would line up in front of the cooler. During the winter, the janitors would carry the cooler and the small stand it rested on from the entryway into the schoolroom and place it near the stove to thaw the solid block of ice that had been formed inside during the night when there was no heat in the building. Since there was no well on the school grounds, the Grants carried fresh drinking water to the cooler in a ten-quart pail from Lenny Griffeth's farmhouse, just a few yards down the hill.

Mom instructed Burnham, Leola and me not to drink from the community mug that sat beside the cooler, but we didn't always follow her instructions. If we took time to retrieve our collapsible tin cups from our lunchboxes or to fold a piece of thick off-white arithmetic paper into a triangular cup for a tiny sip of water, we would be at the end of the line for drinks.

Our impatience might have been the reason we contracted every communicable disease that swept through our school—mumps, measles (red and German), chickenpox, whooping cough, colds, cold sores, the itch, and head lice. The latter two probably were not transmitted from the rim of a drinking cup. Most likely, the lice crawled from hat to hat on the coat hooks or from head to head as we sat close to each other in our double seats sharing books, eating lunches, or sharing secrets.

After drinks it was, of course, time to go to the toilet—not the bathroom or the basement, but the toilet. Separate hallways ten to twelve feet long that opened into one side of the classroom led to the boys' and girls' facilities. The woodshed was located beside the hallway to the boys' toilet with a flimsy partition that afforded little privacy. Each toilet cubicle had one small hinged window directly above the seat. In the spring and early fall, the window was lifted and hooked to a wire hanging from a rafter in the unfinished ceiling. In the winter, the window was closed, but the open spaces around the frame allowed an ample supply of fresh air to blow in and carry with it a fine spray of snow, which piled up in miniature drifts on the toilet seats. Only in dire emergencies would we brave these conditions and we did not waste any time getting back to the classroom.

Mom made this rigorous experience even more severe by insisting we were not to sit on the toilet seats. She was convinced we got "the itch" (a red rash) from the toilets. We didn't understand her logic, since the first symptoms of this disease always appeared between our fingers and on our stomachs, so we ignored this admonition, as we did the one to avoid the drinking cup. We felt we endured enough discomfort going to the toilet with wind-driven snow stinging our posteriors without having to defy gravity by trying to sit poised in midair.

For permission to go to the toilet, we raised our hands and extended either one finger or two to indicate which bodily function we needed to perform. I never figured out why we had to be so specific.

Our teacher, Miss Farrington, moved efficiently and smoothly from one class to another as she listened to recitations and introduced new material first to one, then to another of the eight students in the school. Dozens of books and manuals were stacked neatly on her desk at the front of the room, corresponding to the dozens of lessons she presented each day to her thirty or more students.

The primary grades were seated in rows next to the south windows, which gave them the advantage of enjoying the warm rays of sun on cold mornings before the heat from the stove reached that far side of the room. It was pleasant to sit at our small wooden desks and color pictures the teacher gave us as busywork to do while she worked with the higher grades. By the process of osmosis many of us learned the primary level material that would be introduced later—as in the "ungraded schools" advocated years later as innovations.

At midmorning recess, we resumed the games we had discontinued at the sound of the school bell in the morning. On went the mittens, coats, and hats that became heavy with balls of snow as we played.

Our lunch boxes waited in rows beneath the coat hooks for our noon meal. If family lunches were packed in the same pail, brothers and sisters gathered in seats near each other so they could share. Others sat with close friends or alone. On cold days, our seats were moved into a circle around the glowing stove. Lunch was followed by another recess outside. In the winter, the boys would be ready to use the snow forts they constructed in the morning for snowball wars. Younger girls might make a snowman, using pieces of coal from the ash pile behind the toilets for eyes, nose, a broad-toothed grin and buttons down the front of his "waistcoat."

School resumed after noon recess with lessons for all grades until the afternoon break, when the primary students were allowed to go home. During my first two years of school, however, I stayed and waited until my older brother and sister were dismissed with the upper grades later in the afternoon and we retraced the route of our morning walk to school. Now our lunch boxes held papers of the previous day, marked and graded with bright red-leaded pencil. Usually, the wind was at our backs and the frosty air of the morning had been warmed by a winter sun.

We hurried home, secure in the knowledge that Mom would be there to greet us, our baby sister would be waiting to be rocked and Dad soon would be coming in from his farm chores. There were no latch-key children in our country school. How fortunate we were.

Stranded on a School Bus
By Ron Laing

The year was 1951. I waited at the end of our farmstead driveway in Westfield for school bus No. 7, which would take me to Presque Isle High School. A brisk wind blew icy pellets at my face that felt like pieces of metal stabbing my skin. Already I wished I'd worn a heavier jacket for it was getting colder by the minute.

Winter in Maine can be fun when there is new snow that's great for skiing and sledding, but this day was just cold and blustery—and the bus was late.

The brakes of the big yellow vehicle squeaked to a stop and heavy tire-chains stopped beating the underside of the fenders. I pulled myself up three steps and noticed many students had decided to stay home today, probably since heavy snow had been falling for several hours. Smart move, I thought. That "snow day" thing we hear about nowadays was unknown in Maine in the 1940s and 1950s—school was never called off because of bad weather.

Our bus driver was Mr. Markey, a skinny man who spoke with a French accent. "Good morning, Ron," he said, and closed the doors behind me. Our big bus lurched forward, its chains again beating the undercarriage as I took a seat beside my best friend, Bob Shaw —Harley's boy.

After a couple of miles, we started down country roads in order to pick up elementary school children who rode with us, making a twelve-mile trip to the city twenty miles long. A hefty state snowplow had cleared the road only fifteen minutes earlier, but already heavy, wind-driven snow had created new drifts. Our skillful driver maneuvered the big International through the wind and through the drifting snow.

We stopped at all the usual places to pick up students who were huddling together to stay warm. The vastness of Aroostook's open farmland allows snow to mound high in some places, while in other areas the roadway is almost bare.

I expected the most difficult part of our trip this day would be the Center Line Road. This gravel road passes over a hilly terrain of open land and is usually dreadful in snowstorms. To our dismay the road had not been plowed. Mr. Markey advanced the bus, its powerful engine forcing us through heavy drifts of wind-packed snow. Just then the wind seemed to blow even harder. The tire-chains clanked a forceful rhythm against the frame below our feet. High snowbanks were building on each side of the road, and snow leaped over snow fencing designed to obstruct it.

Ralph Soucier, a senior, and I, an underclassman, were two of the bigger boys on the bus. We made our way to the front to see if we could assist.

"We're sure getting lambasted," said our driver, as he moved us steadily forward into a whiteout wilderness. "I'm having trouble seeing where the road is."

"We'll help you follow the telephone poles," I said.

"That's all we've got. Just the poles. Each drift seems bigger than the one I just went through."

"Looks like the storm is settling in for the night," someone behind us said—but it was only eight-thirty a.m. By now everyone realized our peril—the younger kids were scared.

"Are we going to be okay?" an elementary student asked. An older girl assured her that our bus was one of the largest the school district had and that we'd be fine.

The laboring bus slammed into a huge drift, bigger than any I'd seen this day. We made it through—but I knew the road ahead would probably be even more difficult for it's always bad. However, should we get through this there would be a country store about a mile away where there'd be food and warmth. Just then we slammed hard into a snowdrift. Snow spattered over the hood of the bus and onto the windshield. Our yellow monster shook and fought like a bull at a rodeo, but halfway through we came to a sudden stop.

We were stuck!

Mr. Markey kept the bus motor running so its heaters could keep us warm. I knew he was unsure how long it would be before help arrived. After a time, he turned the motor off to save fuel. Half an hour later he turned it on again. By this time, two and a half hours had passed since I left the farm. I should have been in school long ago.

By noontime no help had arrived. Some opened their lunches, but many, like me, didn't bring lunches—we ate at the cafeteria. Those who had food shared with others. The hours seemed to pass slowly. We were helpless. Back then no one knew what a CB or a cellphone was. The big questions we faced were: Do we have enough fuel to get us through the night if we had to stay that long? What about food? And what about toilet needs? Mr. Markey offered few answers. He was determined to conserve fuel to keep us warm, which he thought was his most important task. Little kids grew more scared, and several cried. Some were hungry again, and others had to go to the toilet. The older girls tried to comfort the ones who cried, but that didn't work for long. After a time, our driver announced if anyone got off the bus for toilet reasons, they must take a high school buddy with them, and they must "stay close" to the bus. Some had to get off, but when the doors opened a few almost lost their desire.

By two in the afternoon no help had arrived and daylight was waning. Mr. Markey discussed with us older boys his strategic plan. It was decided before it got any darker a couple of us would hike the mile or so to the store and bring back blankets and food. By doing this we could inform people we were stranded and let rescuers know where we were.

It seemed a good plan, so Ralph and I said we'd brave the storm. We wrapped ourselves with scarves, put on caps that had earmuffs, and taking extra mittens, stepped into a world of whiteness. Before leaving we'd decided our best assurance for success was simply not to get lost. To accomplish this, we'd go from utility pole to utility pole, the only landmarks we had. But first we'd make a test effort by going only two poles away. This went well, so we pressed on. By the time we got to the fourth pole the wind had picked up so fiercely we had to stop until we could see again, then push on.

I counted the poles—ten so far. An hour later, cold and soaking wet, we saw the lights of the store. How good it was to be warm and to get into dry clothing.

"Our phone is out, but we'll try to get you help," the storeowner told us. He and his wife loaded a toboggan with blankets, food, water, flashlights and batteries—and we started our trip back.

The return trip was not any easier because it seemed much darker. We strained our eyes to see the gray form of the next pole. If we couldn't see it, we didn't move until something became visible—our lives might depend on this. We'd agreed with Mr. Markey before leaving that when the bus was running its headlights would be on and that every five minutes he would blow the horn in an effort to assist us.

After what seemed forever, we heard the horn. When we got to the next pole, we saw lights from our bus. Ralph and I were pleased that everything we'd planned had worked out well.

Everyone was glad to see us and the food we'd brought. We became instant heroes to forty-six kids and a bus driver—for a few hours anyway. Mr. Markey gave us both a friendly slap on the back. "Great job!" he said.

About the time I should be getting home from school that day, a huge State of Maine snowplow approached the rear of our bus. Shouts of joy went up from happy kids. We all watched as the big plow pushed heavy snow away. Two men with shovels dug around our wheels and soon we were free. The plow cleared the road before us all the way to Route 1—but first we stopped at the little store to say "thank you" and to use their bathrooms. By the time we said "goodbye" there were no candy bars left on the shelves.

Our Winter Playground

By Sister Mary Denis (Alene Schwartz)
and Phyllis Schwartz Hutchins

As told by Leonard Hutchins

Santa Claus couldn't have imagined a better winter present than our road to school. It was the road from the Maine-New Brunswick border east of Fort Fairfield to Aroostook Junction, New Brunswick. The Fort Fairfield end of that road is called the Aroostook Falls Road.

For most of the year, it was just five miles of rutty dirt road through evergreen forest. It meandered more than the sheer-sided river gorge, which it more or less followed. A straight railroad track crossed it several times.

During the spring and fall, our square-built 1930s school bus bumped and rattled us to school on time. There was no time to play. Since the seats all faced forward, we could hardly talk to our friends.

However, sooner or later a much-anticipated storm sifted knee-deep snow over our road to school. A town road crew used several teams of horses to pack the snow with a heavy wooden snow-roller. We lived at the end of the road, so the horses pulled the snow-roller in a loop around our farmyard. It returned down the road.

The packed snow smoothed the bumps, but our school bus could not run on it. So Mr. Walker, our bus driver, became a sled teamster, taking us to school in a sled instead of the bus. The school sled was a little house on top of a bobsled pulled by two horses. He couldn't deliver us to school faster than his plodding horses could walk, so the road to school became our winter playground.

The first school-sled day was like a holiday. Dressed in warm home-made clothes, we three sisters and our brother waited in the cold morning darkness until we heard the rhythmic jingle, jingle, jingle of harness bells down the road. Soon the yellow glow of the school-sled window outlined horses' heads bobbing with each jingle. Our sled's straight sides, rounded top, and stove pipe materialized around the window. Cedar smoke drifted above us when Mr. Walker stopped the sled.

We waved to Mom who always watched from our kitchen window. Then we opened the back sled doors to the glow of the kerosene lantern and the smell of the wood stove. The horses plodded forward and we found places for our dinner pails among firewood under the benches that lined the sidewalls. About sixteen students from five or six families rode in the sled.

Mr. Walker often tied the horse reins so they wouldn't slip out through two holes under the front window. He turned around on his front bench beside the stove and talked to us. Horse hooves thumped in snow. Snow squeaked under sled runners. Harness bells jingled. The sled rocked gently. We laughed. Face-to-face seats made talking fun.

In morning twilight, we slid out the doors, ran ahead of our barn-red sled, and visited with waiting neighbor students. With our friends, we walked behind the sled, rode standing on the back runners, ran in crisscross paths to make snow chains in deep snow, and fell backward to wave our arms and legs to make snow angels. When the road veered close to the rim of the river gorge, our bellies felt like twisted mittens. We kept our small friends safely away, and we always made sure little ones were not left behind. From a distance, we children must have looked like a flock of little chicks milling around our mother hen sled.

When we needed a rest, we climbed back into the sled. We dug snow from our boots, warmed feet, dried mittens and helped small friends. The smell of wet wool mixed with smoke from the wood stove and kerosene lantern.

The horses knew the way, so Mr. Walker often slept. He knew we watched out for our younger friends. The horses refused to cross the railroad tracks without their teamster's command, so we often had to wake Mr. Walker at crossings.

When the sled crossed the railroad track, steel horseshoes clanked on the rails. Once in a while, a steel sled runner screamed an ear-splitting screech when it slid over the rails.

Sometimes we had to wait for the train. Its chugs sounded louder when it rumbled closer. The big black engine had churning wheels, a whistle, a smokestack and a snowplow. The snowplow made a long white cloud of swirling snow under the long, black cloud of smoke from the smokestack. It pulled a string of square cars of many colors and a red caboose. The engineer and fireman in the engine room and people in the caboose waved to us.

The steam whistle sounded hollow and blew a cloud of white wisps. It had its own language. Long blasts shouted, "Danger." Two little toots said, "Hi, there." After the train went by, it was fun to run up the track and wait for our sled at the next crossing.

In town, Mr. Walker often stopped at the store so one of us could leave a family molasses jug to be filled. Sometimes we arrived at school

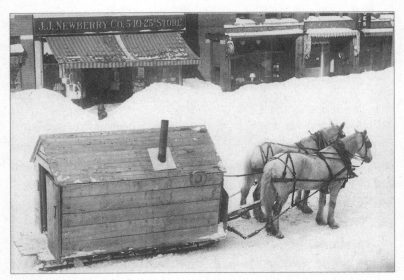

The school sled. Courtesy of Richard Graves.

in time for recess. At noon, we saved bread and biscuits from our lunch. In order to deliver us home in time for supper, our sled left school well before the last bell. Our in-town schoolmates envied us.

If we were lucky, our first stop on the way home was the store. The glass or earthenware molasses jug was very carefully placed under Mr. Walker's bench.

Sometimes one of us had a nickel or dime to spend. The storekeeper was generous, and we shared candy.

The twilight-to-darkness ride home was a moving inside-camping trip. We talked, joked and laughed while we toasted our saved bread and biscuits on the stove. Toast and toasted biscuits never smelled or tasted better. We shared, and we made sure Mr. Walker had some.

When the school sled stopped in our farmyard road loop, we were glad to see Mom in our kitchen window watching for us.

We wish you had been there to share the fun.

Heroes of 1947
By Paul Lucey and Fran Mitchell

Patten Academy was founded in 1847 in the village of Patten, Maine, which was known as "The Jewel in the Wilderness." One hundred years later, "March Madness" gripped the small community at the northern end of Penobscot County. This is the story of how that happened.

Willis R. Phair was the principal and coach who revived basketball after World War II.

In February 1947 (the academy's centennial year) the team accepted an invitation to play in the Eastern Maine Small Schools tournament held in Brewer. In a thrill-packed game Patten Academy defeated Milo High,

37-31, avenging a two-point defeat in the same tournament the previous year. Next came a victory over a Limestone quintet that had beaten a highly rated Washburn team. The victory placed the Patten Eagles in the final game of the tournament against Lawrence High School of Fairfield, a school of 280 students. Patten enrolled fewer than one hundred.

The game was a thriller with Patten fans filling two sections of the old Bangor Auditorium (new one built in 1953). The score see-sawed with basket matching basket and Patten holding on to a one-point lead, 43-42, that won the Eastern Maine Championship and sent the team to the State Championship game.

A long line of cars filled with fans escorted the team to the town square where hundreds more waited to give the heroes a hearty welcome home. The mill whistle blew, the fire sirens shrieked, and horns sounded in the excitement that seized the town during the celebration. There was one more obstacle to overcome. A strong quintet from Class A Gould Academy (250 students) in Lewiston challenged Patten Academy for the State Championship.

Four buses carried students and Patten fans to Lewiston to see the game. The long trip was worthwhile when the Eagles defeated a strong Gould team, 36-33, adding another magnificent plaque to the display case of Maine's new champions. The trophy saluted the contenders for the unofficial New England Championship, giving rise to a boisterous greeting in Patten—ON TO BOSTON.

Alumni and friends of the academy contributed funds to help defray the expenses of the team and the cheerleaders. On March 19, the entire student body and all the grammar school students marched down Main Street to the beat of drums and the tunes of a bazooka band to send the boys off to the "big city."

Fans followed the boys to Boston in a special car attached to a regular passenger train and poured into the Boston Garden. The Patten team was awed for they had never seen such space, nor glass instead of wooden backboards. The Boston Latin band was playing joyfully, for their team would surely win.

About 14,000 spectators expected to witness Boston Latin spank the "upstart" kids from Maine with their team of nine players.

The play was exciting from tossup to final basket. Soon, even the Boston fans were pulling for the scrappy Mainers. Their style of play showed they were well-coached and deserved to be representing their state. At the half, the Eagles had a 12-11 lead. After the half, Boston Latin came back to roll up a 22-15 margin. Some of the Eagle faithful may have been ready to accept a "moral victory" against the school of 1,800 students. "Oh, ye of little faith!"

By the fourth quarter, the lead was cut to two points. With 45 seconds to play, the Boston lead held. Now it was hand-wringing time for the Eagle faint-of-heart. But hold on! Captain Wilson sank a two-pointer in the final seconds to tie the game and send it into a three-minute overtime period.

The overtime play was anticlimactic. The Patten boys had caught the Latin team going down the stretch to give them confidence that carried into the extra time. The Eagles scored five quick points that held up for three minutes to crown them the New England Champions. Close to 14,000 new fans gave the champions a standing ovation as they left the floor.

Albie Booth, famed Yale athlete who was officiating, told a newspaper reporter, "Those are the finest boys I've seen all year. They were gentlemen all the way."

The return home was a series of celebrations honoring the conquering "heroes." In Portland, fans and a band joined news reporters and camera crews to interview the boys and celebrate their victory. The Bangor and Brewer high school students and bands saluted the team with "Patten Academy Will Shine Tonight," causing the boys to choke up with emotion. The Bangor and Aroostook Railroad officials had arranged a wonderful banquet for them and rooms at the Penobscot

Exchange Hotel, as well as a special bus for the trip home. The bus to Patten stopped in each town (Lincoln and Sherman in particular) where students and adults cheered the New England basketball champions.

A tumultuous greeting awaited them by the whole population of Patten and hundreds of people from nearby towns. A cannon roared, sirens shrieked, and bells tolled in tribute to the victorious champions. A flyover from the Houlton air base added to the boisterous scene and streets were renamed after the players.

The townspeople expressed their pride at a testimonial banquet at Founders' Memorial Hall. It was standing room only as Gov. Horace Hildreth and other notable people spoke on behalf of the proud citizens of Maine. The ceremony ended with Coach Phair saying goodbye to his boys as a team and congratulating them for "soaring like Eagles in the Garden's rarefied air breathed by CHAMPIONS." It's the Stuff of Legends!

Note: The Boston Latin coach, Steven Patten, learned from his family that he was the great-great-grandson of Amos Patten, for whom the town was named.

Note: After this game, schools of different classes were no longer allowed to compete against each other.

Winter Shoes
By Glenna Johnson Smith

He was up long before daybreak on that Friday of the third week in January. In the cold of the upstairs chamber he dressed in his only decent school pants—the heavy, dark green melton wool pair that his mother sponged daily and pressed and mended when necessary. Despite his excitement over competing for the first time in the Limestone Winter Carnival, Donny Smith ate his usual breakfast of oatmeal, eggs, homemade bread toasted, and a couple of his mother's big, sugared chocolate doughnuts washed down with several glasses of milk. By six he had pulled on his heavy wool shirt and sweater, home-knit mittens and socks, and cap worn low over his face to ward off the below-zero cold of the pre-daylight morning as he walked the mile and a half to Easton Station.

Donny, a high school sophomore, had decided he wanted to be a snowshoer and compete in carnivals. Skinny and small for his age, he weighed barely a hundred pounds. However, he was strong and wiry from working on Gramp's farm, and he had the determination to be champion; only thing was he didn't have any snowshoes. Then a kind neighbor, Walter Sawyer, lent him some for practice, and he saved up until he could go to Herb Dickey, the local harness maker, and have a pair done to his specifications.

He explained to Mr. Dickey that they had to be small and extra light for racing, but Mr. Dickey, knowing that it was hard for a young fellow to come up with the eight or ten dollars, decided the boy needed good heavy snowshoes that would last him. Disappointed, Don took the new snowshoes under his arm on that cold walk to the station, where he met the other seven boys and Bill Hale, the high school principal and coach of all sports. They huddled around the potbellied stove to warm themselves until the seven o'clock train came steaming and clanking to a halt.

The first leg of the journey took them to Phair Junction, where they circled another station stove for the three-hour wait for the train to Caribou. There they cozied up to yet another stove for another couple of hours, waiting for the train to Limestone. Their mothers had seen to it that they were amply supplied with sandwiches, cookies and doughnuts so they munched while they waited.

By two o'clock they had completed the 22-mile journey and were ready to race in the few remaining hours of daylight. Little Don won his snowshoe races and, as high-point man of the day, was offered a pair of beautiful racing snowshoes. When the merchant donating the prize heard that he had just bought new snowshoes he offered Don skates instead, but Don chose the perfect snowshoes. He knew his sisters could use the heavy pair for visiting their friends, because there were no open roads from the first big snow in November until the men shoveled out in March for town meeting day.

After the meet each Easton boy was taken home by a Limestone boy. They ate supper and then went to the new high school gymnasium for the Carnival Ball, wearing the same clothes they had put on in the morning. They saw a Limestone girl crowned Carnival Queen, and they danced with many girls—maybe even with the Queen if they were lucky. Then they spent the night with their host family, and got up on Saturday to a big breakfast and the long train trip in reverse.

After the Limestone Carnival there were others in the same order each year. The Easton Carnival came after Limestone and then came the big three-day event at Fort Fairfield on the first weekend in February. A ski jump was constructed on Fisher Hill and from there the jumpers could overlook the entire town. This meet included teams from Easton, Fort Fairfield, Caribou, Limestone, Mars Hill and Presque Isle. Qualifying trials were run on Friday and the finals took place on Saturday.

The Bangor and Aroostook Railroad ran special excursion trains and people enjoyed this chance to get out of town in winter as much as they enjoyed seeing the hometown boys race and cheering for the exciting quarter-mile horse races on the frozen Aroostook River. There were always a few townspeople who managed to smuggle flasks on board, so train rides home were likely to be rowdy.

Don's first trip home after the Fort Fairfield Carnival the engineer invited each of the boys, one by one, to ride with him. Don was surprised to find that the engine tossed and bucked like a spirited colt. It was not at all like the smooth ride in the cars, but it was the highlight of that trip.

The carnivals had 100-yard dashes and quarter-mile races for snowshoes and skis, two-mile cross country for skis and one-mile cross country for snowshoes. A medley relay alternated 100 yards on skis and 100 yards on snowshoes for 400 yards. Athletes wore no special clothing in the 1930s. Skiers wore ankle-high boots and the snowshoers wore moccasins, the same ones they wore every day.

After Don broke the state record in the 100-yard dash, it became a foregone conclusion that he would always win that event. So at the time of the Easton Carnival, Bill Hale said to Don's mother, "June, is there anything you need? Don's sure to win a prize, and he doesn't need any more winter's sports stuff."

"Bill, my flatiron just played out. I could sure use a new one!"

An electric iron may have been a strange prize for a high school boy, but Don was glad to win it for his mother.

Presque Isle had the last carnival of the season in mid-March, and the hot sun caused the snow to melt and mix with the winter's manure. After running knee deep in slush, Don recalled that they didn't smell very good as they warmed up at the Carnival Ball! Although winter carnivals continued to be a high point in Don Smith's high school years, perhaps none capped the excitement of that first trip to Limestone. It seemed to him on the ride back to Easton that he had been away for a week. He wanted to run all the way home from the station, feel the warmth of the kitchen, smell the new bread and the beans baking, show the family his new snowshoes, and tell them all about his exciting adventures away from home.

New Sweden Athletes

By Dorothy Anderson

One evening early in the winter of 1931-1932, a group of young men gathered at Aaron Anderson's store in the Bangor and Aroostook section of New Sweden and rode up the hill on the back of Ernest Jacobson's truck to Svea Hall at the Gustaf Adolph Lutheran Church.

"The roads weren't plowed in those days," Edmund Anderson recalled, "but there wasn't enough snow yet that winter to keep some vehicles off the road, especially with a truck body full of strong eager boys who provided traction and who could probably push the truck back on the road if it went off."

Ivar Menton had called a meeting of people interested in forming a ski club in town. Ivar—son of the Lutheran minister, the Reverend Zack Menton—had come over from Sweden to join his family at the Lutheran Church parsonage. He had undertaken three years of specialized gymnastics training in Sweden and had also engaged in competitive skiing and swimming in his native country.

Those were the Great Depression years, and people did not have much money. Few people had jobs and few recreational opportunities existed for those with time on their hands. Although the initial idea was to form a ski club, the group soon became known as the New Sweden Athletic Club, or NSAC. In addition to ski meets, NSAC organized hockey and basketball teams and sponsored summer track meets and recreational activities at nearby Madawaska Lake. And, perhaps unique to Northern Maine, it organized a gymnastics team. But in a part of the country where snow is measured in feet, not inches, winter sports predominated.

Ski historians say cross-country skiing and jumping were brought to this country by Scandinavian immigrants in the mid-1800s. Skiing first came to the western regions of Colorado and Montana, and even the mining camps of California, in the 1850s. On the East Coast, groups such as Norwegian settlers in Northern New Hampshire and Swedes in Northern Maine introduced skiing, first as transportation and then as recreation to Northern New England in the late 1800s.

In 1883, Norwegian and Finnish immigrants to Berlin, New Hampshire, organized the first ski club in the country, the Nansen Ski Club. This club launched many competitive skiers, some of whom went on to form the nucleus of the Dartmouth College Ski Team, the first collegiate ski team in the country. Some of those Nansen skiers went on to compete in subsequent Winter Olympics, and a few, such as Nansen and Dartmouth skier Sel Hannah, made their life work designing ski areas that launched the downhill ski industry both in New England and out West.

Early historical accounts of Northern Maine's Swedish colony make frequent reference to the immigrant children making their way through the snow on "Swedish snowshoes" or *skidor* (long, narrow cross-country skis), traveling as far as five miles through the woods to school. One account describes the first minister in town, Pastor Andrew Wiren, skiing six miles to the settlement at Jemtland to teach school while attending to his pastoral duties during the winter of 1872-1873, two years after the colony's founding.

Children learned to ski almost as soon as they learned to walk, using shaped barrel staves at first, then graduating to long, narrow skis with simple bindings made by people in town. A single pole, often fashioned from a mop or broom handle, was used to help navigate. The skis were two lengths, with long, tapered and sometimes elegantly carved points. The longer ski aided in balance and in negotiating the drifts, since early skiing was truly cross-country without set trails or roads. Children used their skis to get to school, to run errands, and just to play. Skis were a means of transportation for adults as well.

"My mother would think nothing of strapping on her skis to go to the store," Edmund Anderson recalled, "and she never walked anywhere; she always ran. Or she would ski over to a neighbor's to attend a sewing circle."

With the advent of NSAC, skis became more specialized, with narrower skis for cross-country and wider, flatter skis for jumping. Two poles were used for speed and balance, and bindings were not made locally, but ordered to fit the skier. Skiing was done along roads that were rolled in winter for travel by horse and long sleds pulled by teams of horses.

Henry Anderson was perhaps the best known in the state for his skill in making skis. Henry created his own trademark made from a piece of scrap iron into which he carved two skis crossed at their tips with poles as the crossarm, creating an "A" for Anderson. He then chiseled "Anderson's Hand Made Skis—New Sweden, Maine," to create his trademark, which he burned into finished skis. He sold them for a dollar a foot. An ad from Henry's *Kaffe Stugan* store in the 1935 NSAC Winter Carnival program touted "genuine Norwegian and Swedish ski bindings and Dartmouth ski boots." The ad went on, "To enjoy the best in skiing, have skis made to suit your weight and height. Models for touring, slalom, jumping and racing used by experts." Others who made and sold cross-country skis were Ernest Jacobson, Carl E. Johanson, and Lars Stadig.

The club met once a month in the town hall at the Capitol. Monthly dues were ten cents and business meetings were followed by a social with Swedish dancing, games, and refreshments. Musicians who played for dancing included Fritjof Jacobson on the violin, Bob Jacobson on the accordion (the composer of "Aroostook Moon" and other local favorites), and Egon Espling on banjo-ukulele. Edmund's treasurer's book, which spanned the early years until 1941, shows more than one hundred dues-paying members at NSAC's peak in the late 1930s. Young people from surrounding communities of Stockholm, Woodland, and even Caribou also became members.

The group did not have an entirely warm reception in town the first year or two. The minister of one church warned in his forceful Swedish, *Det är ogräs som växar upp ibland oss.* ("There's witchgrass growing among us.") These were hard words for the young organizers to accept, and they set out to prove the group's good intentions by not allowing anyone who had been drinking into the meetings and even voting some members out because they had indulged in alcohol before coming to club-sponsored events.

The club also had members in their forties and fifties who served as boosters, supporting activities in many ways. Businessmen provided financial backing for the teams and middle-aged men and women worked hard on fundraisers for the club. Fritjof (the fiddler at NSAC dances) and Olive Jacobson were active supporters, as were Clifford and Dagmar Anderson, Robert and Dora Westman, Lawrence and Mabel Hemberg, and Broor and Lily Gustafson, among others. Ski-maker and community leader Henry Anderson was the ski team manager, traveling with the team to prepare their skis with wax and applications of tar. Henry Anderson's sister Hildur Anderson was also active in NSAC.

NSAC agreed to provide wood to heat the town hall as payment for the use of the building for its activities in winter. Edmund Anderson recalls buying a cord of wood for six dollars for the club to use in the town hall's massive wood furnace, which would take the better part of a day to warm the building.

NSAC held ski meets with other towns and sponsored winter carnivals beginning in 1933 on Pierson Hill (now Ringdahl Hill) overlooking the B&A section of town. The Pierson Hill became the site for carnivals because of its proximity to the B&A station for those traveling from other towns to attend or compete in the events.

Charlene Olander Espling, a member of NSAC, remembered that her father John Olander's general store was a frequent meeting place for ski team members who often would practice in the moonlight. And just down the road from his store, in front of Aaron Anderson's general store, was the hockey rink, which saw regular use for impromptu games as well as for meets hosted by NSAC's hockey team, the Red Wings.

Ski meets were held in the surrounding towns of Fort Fairfield, Caribou, and Presque Isle, towns which also held winter carnivals. Both men's and women's squads skied in the competitions. Meets were often held on weekdays and were organized around the train schedules. In order to get to the Fort Fairfield winter carnival, New Sweden skiers would take the 7 a.m. southbound train, attend the events from 1 to 4 p.m., return on the northbound train getting back to town by 11 p.m.—and then find their way home (on skis) from the Bangor and Aroostook station. NSAC skiers would usually take top places, notably Walter (Buck) Ostlund, Arvid Jacobson, Allen Kampe, Ernest Anderson, and Carl Johnson.

The first NSAC winter carnival was held on February 25, 1933. A program for the 1936 Fourth Annual Winter Carnival detailed the long day of events, including downhill, slalom, ski jumping, various cross-country races including obstacle and muddle races, and a hockey game against a team from another town. Children's events would take place in the morning and late afternoon, with competitive racing and jumping held in the middle of the day, timed around the northbound train's schedule. The B&A potato houses would be used to put up horses and sleighs as well. A noontime public dinner in the vacant C.J. Tornquist store was a club fundraiser. In the evening townspeople would fill the town hall for a basketball game, the crowning of the carnival queen, and a dance.

NSAC built a ski jump in the early years on the upper part of the Pierson Hill. The maximum jump was 75 feet, although 40 to 50 feet was more typical. Because the landing was not a long one, jumpers would have to execute a clean, sweeping turn at the bottom, ending up facing the hill. Today, that turn is popularly known as the Telemark Turn which, along with new developments in skis and bindings, has revolutionized downhill skiing, bringing Alpine skiing closer to its

Nordic roots. Some of the timber used to build the framework for the jump was purchased in Canada and hauled from Edmundston, New Brunswick, down to New Sweden by Ernest Jacobson, a local woodworker and competitive skier.

The skis used for jumping were flat and easier to make than cross-country skis, which required a knack for shaping the ski using the natural camber of the wood. Jumping skis were wider and heavier, with three lengthwise grooves in the bottom, rather than the single groove on the racing ski. These jumping skis were made by a number of people in town, including Edward Anderson who made skis for family and friends.

Fort Fairfield had a larger jump and their skiers, members of the White Bunny Ski Club, excelled in jumping. Even the tiny village of Jemtland had a small ski jump on Hedman Hill, but no competitions were held there (although Jemtland held its own local carnival for a few years).

Snowshoeing was also an event at the meets and carnivals. Stanley Pierson, who also snowshoed for the Caribou High School Winter Sports Team, took the state title in the mile race for snowshoeing.

Cross-country ski marathons held in the winters of 1936 and 1937 from Bangor to Caribou and another year from Riviere-du-Loup, Quebec, to Caribou were organized by a one-time NSAC member, Swedish-born Bob Johnson, who took first place in 1936. The club sponsored several members, among them Buck Ostlund, Laverne Anderson, and Harold Bondeson, who skied and placed in these grueling 170-mile marathons which took four days. Walter Stadig, a Swede living in Soldier Pond, was in his fifties when he finished in fifth place one year.

In 1937, Fort Fairfield's White Bunny Ski Club held a tri-town Ski Race from Fort Fairfield to Presque Isle to Caribou and back to Fort Fairfield—a thirty-five mile loop which skiers repeated on three consecutive days. NSAC's Laverne Anderson took first place with Alden Anderson in second place.

Although skiing was a natural highlight of the NSAC, basketball and hockey teams were formed after the first year and competed with teams from other towns.

Adeline Anderson Ekman was on the women's basketball team and was its manager in 1936. She remembered the women's team traveling to Stockholm with the men's team for competitions via a long sled covered in hay.

"It was a slow trip on a freezing winter night," she recalled, "but those rides never seemed long or cold to us."

In the summers, an all-male gymnastics team practiced weekly under the instruction (in the Swedish language) of Ivar Menton. Activities included tumbling and other floor exercises, building four-tiered human pyramids, boxing, and marching routines, which Menton would count out in Swedish *Avdelning, Halt, En, Två* ("Detachment, Halt, One, Two") to signal the end of the routine. The team put on several public exhibitions in the town hall, followed by a Swedish dance. It also held a banquet and exhibition for town leaders and their wives.

NSAC leased a lot at Madawaska Lake for fifteen dollars a year for other summer activities. Club members built a float with a diving tower and members could put up tents and camp out. Edmund Anderson and Charlene Espling remembered camping there on different occasions, sometimes with a tent for a group of young women set up alongside a tent for young men. They insisted that "nothing went on" between the two tents except a lot of giggling and pranks. Swim and track meets, hot dog roasts, and other socials were sponsored by the club.

NSAC teams wore all-white suits, one for summer gymnastics and a winter suit for ski events, consisting of a white jacket, pants, and a navy cap with the NSAC emblem. Wilbert Anderson skied slalom races competitively for the club. His suit is on display at the New Sweden Museum, along with a number of sets of locally made skis.

Membership in the athletic club declined after 1941 as young men left town, first for factories in Massachusetts that produced war materials and then for military duty in World War II. The club was dissolved by 1942.

Organized skiing activities continue in New Sweden. For several decades the Health Council sponsored a winter carnival at the school, with races for schoolchildren and adults. Since 1976 the Henry Anderson *Ski Dag*, now a part of the Caribou Winter Carnival, has attracted racers of all ages. NSAC skier Ralph Ostlund, Buck's younger brother, won in the master's category, aged 70 and over, in the 1997 Henry Anderson Memorial Ski Race. And Henry's great-granddaughter, Haley Jepson, won in the 13-and-under category representing a new generation of New Sweden athletes.

As the World Watched
By Kathryn Olmstead

With an athlete from Stockholm as the only Maine native in the 2014 Olympics in Sochi, Russia, in February, and with teams from twenty-nine countries converging on Presque Isle for the 2014 World Youth/Junior Biathlon Championships in March, Aroostook County began 2014 on the world stage of biathlon competition.

The Maine Winter Sports Center, with world-class ski venues in Presque Isle and Fort Kent, has attracted several international championship competitions since its founding in 1999. Dedicated to restoring skiing as a way of life in Northern Maine, MWSC has inspired local schoolchildren as well as athletes from across the nation.

Russell Currier of Stockholm was one of those schoolchildren. At first a reluctant eleven-year-old participant in the MWSC Healthy

Hometowns Program, Currier was soon hooked on skiing. Through victory and defeat, he learned persistence. From high-school cross-country ski championships he advanced to World Cup competition, skiing in Finland, the Czech Republic, Italy, and other sites. In 2014, his dream became reality when he was named to the four-member U.S. Olympic Biathlon Team in mid-January. His home community erupted with excitement and hustled to put together a benefit supper at his alma mater, Caribou High School, raising enough money to send his parents, Debbie and Chris Currier, to Sochi to watch their son compete.

As Olympians were departing from Sochi in February, biathletes from around the world were beginning to arrive in Presque Isle for the 2014 International Biathlon Union Youth/Junior World Championships at the Nordic Heritage Ski Center. Teams from Russia and Austria were the first to arrive, allowing two weeks to practice on the rigorous trails at the center. By February 27, they had been joined by more than 400 biathletes, coaches, staff and family members from Europe, Asia, Latin America, New Zealand, England and Canada for opening ceremonies at the Gentile Recreation Center at the University of Maine at Presque Isle.

The national flags that identified the teams as they paraded into the ceremony also added color to the competition at the Nordic Heritage Center February 28 though March 7. Amid a cacophony of cowbells and dynamic music, fans, bundled up to their eyeballs against icy cold wind, cheered skiers as they displayed their marksmanship from prone and standing positions and sped around the race course to a finish in front of the stands.

Armies of volunteers in red parkas performed the myriad tasks required to meet the high standards of the International Biathlon Union. Technical record keeping on the shooting range, timing, trail maintenance, food service, communications, transportation, sanitation, media management, tech support and accommodations are just a few of the responsibilities fulfilled by volunteers from the community, many of whom have gained experience in past events.

"Our communities have mobilized over four hundred dedicated volunteers and been months in preparation for the IBU, biathletes, coaches, support staff and, most of all, spectators and fans to arrive and enjoy our venue," said event director Jane Towle. "It has been a privilege to work with the volunteers who have skillfully planned and executed this tremendous event, one which will showcase Aroostook County at its best to the world."

Secret Pleasure
By *Jenny Radsma*

A spring snowstorm is forecast for tomorrow and already I can feel the stir of excitement within me. At work someone says it will start to snow after lunch, but the online weather service predicts the eight inches of snow slated for our area won't begin until dusk.

By supper time on the forecast day, still no sign of snow. Later, reading in my chair, I glance outside with each page I turn. A snow squall starts. "Here it comes," I think to myself, but it peters out as quickly as it started. At 9 p.m. the low overcast sky makes plucking the snow by hand seem almost possible, but an hour later, still the promised snow remains absent so I go to bed. "Probably another forecast the meteorologists got wrong," I tell myself. I'm reluctant to let go of the secret sense of energy and thrill I get from a storm.

When the alarm goes off for my early morning exercise class, a light snow is falling. From the glow of the streetlight, I can see that a slim white blanket, just a couple of inches at best, covers the driveway. However, when I return home an hour later, with daybreak hidden behind the clouded sky, my earlier footsteps are all but filled in. I glance at the kitchen clock: I have just enough time to clean the driveway before breakfast. Although I walk more than I drive in the small town where I live, I like to keep a shipshape driveway. I tell others it's because of the work ethic with which I was brought up, that it's pride in keeping my home looking trim. And while those explanations are certainly true, the larger truth is that I simply love to clear snow—from the driveway, the patio, the front porch, and from the roof. Unlike my parents who shoveled their own and the neighbor's sidewalk, it's just my own walkway on which I focus—double-wide and three cars in length as it is. And now there's enough snow to make removing the snow a worthwhile effort.

With the comparatively mild temperature, I'll be fine with the jacket I have on. I need only to don the hightop boots I keep just for this job. The overhead motion light flicks on as I shovel out the snow in front of my garage. The snow is moisture-laden and heavy, so I decide to use the blower. I fiddle with the switches, plug in the start switch, then nudge it into action. As the engine roars to life, I hold my breath for the inevitable burst of smelly exhaust that disperses into the air.

After easing the snowblower out of the garage, I begin the center cut, aiming the snow chute to one side, watching a perfect plume of snow arc its way over the bank that outlines the edge of the driveway. The stripe forming behind me fills me with delight when I glance back to see the straight even lines on each side. At the mouth of my driveway, I scramble to cut through the mass of snow left by the snowplow while at the same time redirecting the snow so as not to cover my neighbor's car. As I crank the chute around, the snow splashes out in front of me onto the freshly plowed road, finally landing on the mound of snow on the other side that at this time of year takes on iceberg-like proportions.

With the "hard stuff" done, I steer the snowblower to clear the next swath of snow up the length of my driveway. With as much daylight as the gray sky allows, I no longer need the streetlight to see that the snowfall is getting heavier. Already the initial black asphalt stripe is cottoned with fresh snow. I go down the length of the driveway, then back up again, each time leaving a widened wake of cleared pavement. With each turn, I toggle the chute to send the snow to the opposite side of the snow-banked driveway. All too soon, I'm done, with just the trimming left to do.

I park the snowblower, then reach for the shovel with mittened hands. I feel the thick snowflakes melt against the heat of my cheeks. My hair is wet and matted with snow because I pulled off my toque some time ago; the cold of melting snow trickles down my neck. Now I open the neck of my jacket to cool off even more. Impulsively, I stick out my tongue to catch the falling snow and suck on it as if it were nectar. I wave as someone drives by and, from elsewhere, I hear the tell-tale "beep-beep-beep" of snow removal equipment backing up.

Aware that I must get ready for work, I reluctantly scurry to finish up. Pushing the shovel in rhythmic, even strokes along where asphalt merges into snow, I scrape up the remnants of snow and hurl them over the snowbank. If I had more time, I'd take the snow scoop and even out the unruly tracks left from the snowblower on the road. Nonetheless, the final picture is what gives me untold satisfaction—a uniform, orderly appearance for my driveway, now banked with clean, sparkling snow.

While shaking off my outerwear before stepping into the house, I notice a tattered spot. Smoothing it out with the shovel, I hear the "pee-be-dee-dee-dee" of a black-capped chickadee in a nearby tree as much as telling me it, too, relishes the splendor of this wintry spring day. Once indoors, I can't help myself: through the kitchen window I take another look at my handiwork and my eyes pan over the pristine, untrammeled snow lying over the front lawns of the neighborhood.

I know I'm meticulous about keeping my driveway clean; some might even call me obsessive. In fact, my neighbor teases me that he thinks I secretly come out at night to vacuum it. What he and others can't appreciate is that with each ribbon of snow I clear, whether by snowblower or shovel, my spirit is calmed and for just that moment, I experience a joy that goes to my bones—for just that moment, I know that all is right with the world.

Before I turn on the radio to hear about the strife in the world, I take a last glimpse through the window at the work of my hands. By the end of the day, the snow that has yet to fall will have turned to mush from the warming sun and the salt on the roadways. But I've had my meditation of labor and because of it, I'm ready for the day that lies ahead.

A Night at the Vaughan House
By Elizabeth Rundlett Pray Hull,
transcribed By her daughter, Jane Beckwith

My mother wrote down her "Great Uncle Owen stories" with her grandchildren and great-grandchildren in mind. Her two great-grandchildren live in Florida and have never, yet, experienced a Maine winter. This is why she took pains to set the scene for what she called "My Favorite Story of Uncle Owen's Vaughan House." Uncle Owen was really her great-uncle, Owen E. Blackden, a brother of her grandmother, Arvilla Blackden Rundlett. This is the kind of story my grandfather loved to tell. Probably her facts and figures reflect his storytelling as much as they do real conditions. Was it Mark Twain who said, "Never let the truth stand in the way of a good story?"

Caribou is in Aroostook County. That far north the winters are cold and long, with much snow. It was not unusual to have a morning temperature of fifty degrees below zero, and snowfalls of three to five feet were commonplace.

In those days (1925) there were no snowplows. Instead, each town used snow-rollers. It took a team of four big workhorses to draw a set of rollers, which were heavy wooden cylinders that must have been five or six feet in diameter. With two rollers side by side on one axle, they would roll a swath ten to twelve feet wide and reduce three feet of snow to a passable roadway. The drivers would start out when a storm started and work in shifts until it ended.

One afternoon in midwinter a new customer checked in at the Vaughan House. He was a "drummer," a traveling salesman, and this was his first trip to Aroostook. A storm was in the air, and he was glad to be inside early. The huge, rambling building was hard to heat in the winter; (by today's standard we'd probably say "impossible!") but the lobby's fieldstone fireplace with its blazing logs was a welcome sight to any guest. Uncle Owen enjoyed playing the part of genial host, welcoming drummers on each return as if they were long-lost relatives, and any newcomers were soon feeling "right to home." So it was a small, friendly group that gathered around the hearth that evening as the wind blew and snow drifted outside the doors.

When it was time to retire for the night, guests would find the temperature in their rooms a chilling shock after the warmth of the fireside. Uncle Owen was unusually generous in providing extra blankets.

This particular newcomer was not accustomed to the winter winds finding their way into his sleeping quarters. Try as he would, he could not get to sleep. In spite of the extra blanket, he shivered and shook.

Along about midnight, with one of the blankets wrapped around him, he went down to the lobby and settled into one of the big leather chairs. Resting his head back and stretching his feet toward the warm hearth, he was soon fast asleep.

The road crews, who had been out in the storm most of the night rolling roads, knew they would find a warm place to rest at Uncle Owen's before returning home. So sometime before daylight, the drummer was awakened by the sounds of snow being stomped off work boots.

He sat up to see two men with frost in their beards. They were busy pulling off gloves and flapping their arms to help warm themselves.

When they turned to look at him, he exclaimed, "My gawd, what room did they put you in?"

The Scandinavian Way
By Kristine Bull Bondeson

I come from a long line of knitters. When I was growing up in a large family in Washburn, Maine, winter evenings and Saturdays (we did not knit in summer or on Sundays, but more of that later) were often taken up with knitting. My grandmother Nettie Rose (Fox) Bull knit in the English style, casting her yarn along with a quick thrust of the right hand, as if feeding a fish line into a swift stream. Steady, smooth, rhythmic. Comforting.

My mother, Edith Colin Bull, demonstrated a style which I later learned was uncommon to most American knitters. Hers was a Scandinavian way of holding the yarn with the tension over the left index finger and along the palm. She would then push the right needle tip into the left and with a gentle click, grab the loop off the finger and repeat it all over again, hands deftly turning like greased cogs. Swift.

At Grandma's we didn't knit on Sunday or play games or cook either, because that was the Sabbath and one didn't do anything that suggested work or play. Knitting was winter work because summer was replete with outside farm work including tending crops and livestock, picking berries, planting and tending the garden, and doing laundry. On rainy days there was putting up food, sewing, ironing, cleaning the house and mending. So it was Saturdays in bitter or wintry weather when we would knit at home or at Grandma's. Grandma and Mom were both exceedingly clever in turning out finely knit mittens and rugged socks for family, friends, and church projects. Coming into Grandma's farm kitchen from her east-facing porch, we'd stamp our snowy feet on the rug, shed our outer garments and hang them on hooks along the wall to the barn. Then we'd clothespin our snow-balled mittens to a wire stretched across the girth of the friendly Home Comfort cookstove.

Both Grandma and Mom used two-ply worsted wool—no acrylic fibers in use back then—in dark but rich browns, greens, blues or cranberry reds, the better to hide any dirt we might encounter when playing outside. Usually their wool came from the Briggs & Little Yarn Company of York Mills, New Brunswick, a brand commonly found in yard-goods or general stores. It came in scores of colors and was bought by the skein, which required winding into a ball. A homey scene comes to mind of my father reclined in his chair with his arms bent at the elbow holding the skein while Mom wound the wool into two coconut-sized balls. Whenever I got a chance to wind, she'd always admonish—"Not too tight!" As she well knew, a tightly wound ball would ruin the yarn's natural elasticity. The Bull women who taught me how to knit mittens always recommended a long wrist (the better to keep from exposing tender skin to low temps) and two or three bands of contrasting color on the wrist (great for reducing squabbles about whose was whose). Practical.

Now that I have arrived at middle age, I look back on those grow-ing years in the 1950s and 1960s and think of all the mittens Mom and Grandma churned out to protect all the little hands. Theirs were perfect little pieces of wearable art. Mom had a five-foot by three-foot by two-foot chest that she filled with knit mittens and socks from one year to the next—empty in January and filled by December. When I was about six, Grandma knit me a pair of lace gloves out of red crochet cotton. In my mind they are perfect, delicate, and special because as daughter number eight, child number eleven and therefore someone used to hand-me-downs, they were new and they were *mine*.

My own style of knitting is a blend of all I've been taught and gleaned along the way. Despite all the charm of the fancy man-made yarns, I still gravitate to wool. My preference is Icelandic since the thick wool makes for fast sweater-knitting and easy felting for wool mittens. Last winter, I fashioned a pair of work mittens for my husband, a farmer who needs the warmth of a felted mitten when doing winter chores, but wants fingers free to fiddle with gears and such. My challenge was to use my old pattern, but to give the mittens a "fliptop." After some fiddling, this I accomplished, then cut up an old suede purse to cover the palms, giving them a handy steering wheel grip. Somehow, (unfortunately, I didn't write down exactly what I did) I achieved fliptop "grip-ability" but my husband's scent made them palatable to the dog and sadly one mitten was chewed. So, assessing the damage, I removed the suede, mended the chew holes, rewashed and dried to felt the repair and re-attached the suede. All better. But they do look a little funny.

Thanks to Mom, Grandma, and my sister Linda (Bull) Davis, I am able to create (and in some cases deconstruct and remake) whatever yarn adventure my heart desires. Every time I teach someone to knit, I think to myself, I am passing along know-how of a craft that stretches back through the centuries. At Christmas, some of my tree decorations include a few homemade mittens and socks in child sizes tied together with a piece of yarn. They were made by my mother and me for my son Finn when he was a toddler. Some have a blowout here or there, but when I look at them, I remember not only the small, tow-headed boy, but also the cozy winter knitting, the skein of yarn Dad holds for Mom as she winds, the delicate red lace gloves, the mittens drying behind the Home Comfort stove, the click of needles, the love of the craft.

Knitters all, carry forward!

Yarn over.

Night Flight

By Linwood Lawrence

Even though I had flown many missions as a Marine pilot during the war, I was shaken one winter night by a frantic call from a father whose wife had phoned that their house deep in the Maine woods was on fire. The phone went dead before she could tell him their children were safe.

Fire at night, in the wintertime, miles from help surely can sound the alarm button in the heart of a parent, especially when the safety of a young family is involved. The year was 1946 and I had recently been placed on inactive duty with the Marines. Our country had survived five long years of war where air power had been the deciding factor. Everyone was very air-minded, especially in emergencies.

On this day, the father had left his camp on Bowlin Pond near Patten early in the morning to buy Christmas gifts. It was a long journey to and from the nearest town as he had to travel many miles over rough woods roads behind a team of horses. Now he wanted somebody to reach his family quickly. His request was for me to fly to his camp.

Even now, nearly five decades later, I remember agonizing over the decisions that had to be made. The unknowns were many, the facts were few. The airplanes I had been used to flying in the Marines were equipped with the latest flight instruments to guide a pilot day or night through any kind of weather. Civilian airplanes were not equipped for night flying. Would the ice of Bowlin Pond be covered with snow? Should the flight be attempted in an airplane equipped with wheels or skis? Could we even find the right pond?

Jerry Bradbury, a former Air Force pilot and friend, offered to accompany me. I happily accepted his offer. Teamwork, another pair of eyes, and sharing the unknowns with a friend always are welcome, especially at night.

As we approached the general area, the glowing fire of the burning cabin identified the pond. We circled and touched down on bare ice. Fortunately, the strong winds following a recent snowstorm had blown the pond clean. We congratulated each other for having selected wheels instead of skis, which would have made landing on ice more treacherous.

After a short walk though the woods, we came upon a "hovel" (a log enclosure for horses). In the dim glow of a timeworn barn lantern, we found a frightened mother anxiously clinging to her two small children. She was understandably nervous as two men she had never seen before approached out of the darkness. Her uneasiness vanished when she realized we had come to help. She asked how we knew about the fire and was relieved to learn that her message had reached her husband before the fire cut off the telephone.

All five of us soon became fast friends. The mother expressed her concern and appreciation for the risks we had taken as she thanked us repeatedly for flying to their rescue. We assured her we would stay with them until her husband returned.

It was long after midnight when her husband finally arrived. His anxiety melted into sheer happiness at finding his family safe. It was a joy to be present for that reunion.

Our return flight was uneventful, but it was hard to concentrate on anything but the events we had just witnessed. Our anticipation of warm beds awaiting at home was interwoven with admiration for the strength of this loving family and how they would pull together to overcome the tragedy of losing their home at Christmas time.

When the media learned about the fire, the hazardous night flight and a family living in a stable, the Christmas spirit touched many hearts. Gifts poured in to be flown to the family. It was a flight I was eager to make. There was only room for one pilot with all the gifts!

When I returned in daylight, to my horror, I found this small pond was surrounded by high ridges. My first thought—How had we made that circling approach to the landing without dragging our wheels through those tall trees?

All pilots know, "Night approaches over unlighted obstructions are disaster in waiting." Perhaps like the first Christmas, the stars were extra bright for us and the huddled family.

The Last of the First
By Gordon Espling

Visualize an elderly heavy-set woman with wooden matches in hand carefully setting flame to small tallow candles on a newly cut Christmas tree drawn from the nearby woods. That is my most impressive and lasting memory of my maternal grandmother, Agnes Clase Anderson, the last surviving member of the original fifty-one men, women, and children who migrated to a new beginning in New Sweden, Maine, in July 1870. This God-fearing mother of eight was dedicated to family and church.

I was of single-digit years, bedridden with a childhood illness that Christmas in the 1930s, yet I was alert to the bustle in the kitchen and anxiously awaiting the evening of festivities and gifts. Grandma lighting the candles on the green tree signaled the beginning, even though the small tapers had to be extinguished soon. Kerosene lamps and larger candles decorating windows and tables continued the illumination. Electricity had not been introduced to the New Sweden farmhouse.

The holiday lasted for an all-too-short period, but the scene is indelible. Swedish tradition demands an extended family gathering on Christmas Eve. There was the evening meal with *lutefisk* and a bounty of foods spread out on a table-to-eternity in the large elongated kitchen. In later years we held similar gatherings of the entire family, spouses, and offspring.

In the pre-dawn hours of Christmas Day, the entire family trudged up the hill through the snow for the *Jul-Ötta* service at the Lutheran Church. In days before my time, Grandma had served as church organist and choir member. She led the winter-worship pilgrimage and then, on the return, supervised the morning meal preparation.

Agnes Anderson was four when her parents, Capt. and Mrs. N.P. Clase, embarked from Sweden with the colonists gathered by William Widgery Thomas. One of her unforgettable memories was climbing up the long slender ladder from the ship anchored in the harbor in Halifax, Nova Scotia. On occasion, Grandma would relate memories of the overland trip to the international boundary at Fort Fairfield, thence to Caribou. The trip had been hard. Her infant sister, Hilma, had died at sea and her burial was the first religious service when the colonists arrived in New Sweden.

Grammie told of the few times she was allowed to accompany her parents to Caribou for an infrequent shopping trip. It was a woods-walk or a ride by horse and wagon to get to town, and the frugal Swedes would barter and spend wisely for food and clothing.

Grammie Anderson spoke with utmost reverence and respect for her father and mother. She delighted in telling us younger children how Captain Clase had been involved as a sea captain in smuggling salt and other staples to China. Because he was convinced a Norwegian sailor had leaked information and caused his ship to be seized, he was ever after suspicious of Norwegians. As she told the story, she let me examine and tenderly lift the salt-stained pages of his Swedish pocket-sized Bible, which she cherished. It was the only material item, except his clothes that he brought home from that voyage.

In hindsight, I wonder where she found hours enough to accomplish the endless tasks of her farm life. As she moved from pantry to stove to sink, she assigned unquestioned chores to young and old farm residents. I got the milking chores morning and evening and I regularly cranked the cream and milk separator. She kept a careful eye when I was allowed to turn the wooden butter churn.

I see her now at the large counter working the soft butter in a wooden bowl, placed in ice to speed the hardening. She added salt, extracted whey (water), placed the butter in a mold and stored the product in the cool cellar. A youngster's reward for work was golden-yellow butter applied generously to fresh rye bread taken from the oven of the wood stove at just the right time.

She was fondly known as "Auntie" by neighborhood children and many often found love and solace in her arms. Thus, we had an endless circle of playmates. She was temperate but firm. Young and old alike would flee her occasional wrath, as when the men returned from a trip to Caribou on the electric car (Aroostook Valley Railroad), their breath heavy with spirits, having neglected to purchase the necessary foodstuffs. Ever the innocent, I found refuge in the bedroom.

The original family log house that was her lifetime residence long remained derelict and empty at the foot of the hill where the settlers arrived and offered prayer under the leadership of W.W. Thomas. I was there in the late 1930s when electricity was wired into the structure. Grammie accepted this change with some apprehension. I watched her from the bedroom window one spring day when the main highway (Maine Route 161) was first opened by a massive state snowplow. She saw many changes in her lifetime, but was ultimately willing to adapt.

The hard, rural life began to take a toll. She developed diabetes, but was able to persevere, although she was unable to handle the insulin injections. Gangrene developed in her foot and I watched in awe as she applied daily dressings to the open wound. Local doctors prescribed amputation, or the prognosis was six months to the grave. She steadfastly refused, and, with unfaltering Christian faith, determination, and selfcare, she outlived at least one respected internist who forecasted her early demise.

Välkommen (Welcome) was the traditional greeting for the parade of friends who frequented the homestead. Beset with failing eyesight and health, she delighted in these visits, and I considered myself a favorite as I was drawn into the circle to listen to her.

In 1946, a national magazine in Sweden pictured Grammie on its cover sipping steaming hot black coffee from a saucer. The photo was not staged. It was Grammie in a typical pose, one I like to mimic. That interview and another by *National Geographic* went on for hours.

Her memory remained keen and accurate and she was ever cheery and alert as she grew older. She could give directions on how to hang the smokehouse ham for curing or question if the green beans had been picked, cut, salted, and packed for the winter. She continued to knit and stitch for need and gift.

Death was kind to Grandma Anderson. It came swiftly one February night in 1949. When the phone call came to our Caribou home, we hastened to her bedside, but not in time. She slept peacefully. Her death ended an era. She was a pioneer who had instilled a sense of values in children, grandchildren, and others who touched her life. She left lasting impressions. Agnes Clase Anderson was the last of the first.

Mysteries of March in Maine
By Jeanette Kennedy Baldridge

In the long winter's night that is February, something stirs in the air—not quite a promise, but a prophecy that it will not always be like this. Here in Maine, by the end of February, when winter is not fun anymore, we need a prophecy like that to believe in. Anticipation of a snowstorm, so thrilling in December with its capacity to transform even the most common, is now dreaded. Houses have become prisons for many who suffer from that hateful affliction, "cabin fever."

White fortresses that have enclosed the roads during December and January are now dirty and gray, squatting like ugly toads. Ski trails are crusty, snow ice cream has lost its charm, and the woodpile is reduced to toothpick material. Something has got to get us through.

Then March arrives, just in the nick of time, the first evidence of the prophecy coming to pass. Dark patches spread out in the icy dooryard, icicles begin to drip and one by one crocuses peek through the snow in surprising bursts of color. Seed catalogues appear in the mailbox, and thoughts turn away from winter toward sunshine, warm earth and seeds to sow.

Yes, there is evidence that winter's on the wane, but spring is not yet. It is not time to put away the woolen mittens and long johns. Backing up to the wood stove is still the first order of business when coming in from outdoors, and ice fishing houses cling tenaciously to their frozen foundations, hugging the ice as if sheer endurance will hold back the approaching sunshine.

Ice fishing houses are reminders to me that I'm "from away." They're not unique to Maine, of course, but they are a wonder and a puzzle to someone from New Mexico. There is more than distance between Maine and the Southwest. When we moved here twenty years ago, I suffered acute culture shock. Maine seemed an alien world after too many years of sagebrush and tumbleweeds.

Language, among other things, was somewhat of a barrier. Although we all spoke English, I was never quite sure what the natives were saying to me. Was there a difference between "bean-hole beans" and "L.L. Beans?" "Cunnin'" was a mystery and "wicked cunnin'" worse yet. And how did one distinguish between "up street" and "down street?" And "over street" was incomprehensible.

I had never eaten lobster. What a thrill that first one was, served up with corn-on-the-cob on a real working pier among the fishermen as they unloaded their boats. New Mexico has many wonderful things, but lobster isn't one of them. Nor does it have anything like the moss-covered stone walls zigzagging through Maine, a kind of infrastructure holding things together. Over the years I've become more or less accustomed to the extraordinary and wonderful things here that most natives take for granted—maple syrup, wild blueberries, and forests carpeted with fern and lady's slippers. But occasionally I am still jarred by something that doesn't fit into my frame of reference. This happens every time I drive past a frozen lake populated with little houses.

The first winter here I wondered about them. There were similar houses in the West, but they were called outhouses and sat out back next to the barn. Something told me these weren't the same thing, and wasn't I surprised when I discovered that people were fishing inside them. I just couldn't imagine such a thing. Fishing inside a house? Even the words "fishing" and " house" seem to contradict each other like "wicked good" or "pretty ugly."

This has taken some adjustment in my sense of "reality," because I'm no stranger to fishing. I started young, tagging along behind my father while he fished the little trout streams of the Colorado Rockies just across the New Mexican border. I had my own pole—a stick with a string and a bent safety pin hook—and whenever he stopped to fish, I plunked in my line beside his. I even caught a few fish with that contraption.

By the time I graduated to a real pole, I was hooked on fishing. It gets into the blood. There's a deep satisfaction in pitting your skill against a fish, in watching the shadows deepen into a purple haze as day drifts into twilight, in listening to the water churn and bubble as it rushes on to places unknown.

My experience of fishing has been many things. I even remember a time when my father took me into Colorado and chopped a hole in a frozen lake through which we could fish. But I have never fished inside a house. So a ghostly village sitting in the middle of a frozen lake jars my sense of reality.

The question that haunts me is this—are they really fishing in those little houses? And if they are, why? What's the motivation? There's no gurgling brook to listen to, no clouds to watch changing shape overhead, no reel to get line tangled in. There isn't the challenge of casting into that perfect spot. Some of my most entertaining moments have come from trying to figure out how to get my husband's favorite lure out of the tree across the stream. There just doesn't seem to be much to do inside those houses.

It occurs to me, however, that maybe I'm missing something. Maybe ice fishing is so popular precisely because it is inactive—a peaceful cocoon with the world and its problems shut outside. Maybe Maine is peopled by philosophers who meditate inside ice fishing houses instead of on mountaintops. After all, aren't most fishers really philosophers? My most profound insights have come while sitting on a riverbank. The outside world fades away and the pole with its line reaching to the unknown becomes an extension of my self. It's as if that pale blue monofilament line is a finger on the pulse of something much larger than my life or the fish's. In those moments, fishing becomes a meditation, a prayer, an inner exploration of the place where all truth resides.

And so, to all you anglers who are spending these last few weekends inside those little houses before they have to be put away for another year, I say, "go for it." I would be the last to find fault with any kind of fishing even if I don't understand it.

For now, with February's prophecy beginning to unfold, I am content planning my garden and watching the snow recede from the black ribbons of asphalt that twist their way through Maine. Well, maybe not quite content. I must confess I'm anxious to wet a line. That time is just around the corner. Soon the snow and ice-fishing houses will be only a memory.

Soon . . . but not yet. Everything in its time, and this is the time for March.

Spring Peepers
By Lana M. Robinson

After another seemingly endless Maine winter, everyone starts getting anxious for the first hints of spring. For many children, the new season is signaled by bare ground on which they can ride their bikes and play baseball. For the elderly, it's the first chance to go outside again without fearing a fall on the ice. For others, it's the smell of fresh air, bedding that has been dried on the clothesline, or mud. All these signs make me confident that spring is right around the corner, but it never officially arrives until I hear the peepers, those noisy heralds whose official name, *Pseudacris crucifer*, is longer than they are.

Last spring, I had been listening for them, straining for them for a few weeks, but to no avail. On April 28, I was returning from one of those meetings that go on forever but get nowhere. With a dull headache, I got out of the car in our yard and plodded toward our house when I stopped dead in my tracks.

"What's wrong?" my husband asked.

"Shh. Listen," I said.

"What is it?"

"Shh!" I repeated. All of a sudden we were surrounded by the chorus of the peepers. Though the night was cool, I couldn't go inside. I had to soak in the joyous music with which they seemed to be celebrating that, like us, they had survived five months of cold and sleet and early darkness. That night, like all the following ones for the next few weeks, I had to have the bedroom window partly open so the peepers could sing me to sleep as they had when I was a child visiting my grandparents on their small dairy farm.

Every night after my grandmother had finished her many chores, she would take me with her on a walk to visit her brother and his family who lived about one-half mile away. Having only her flashlight to guide us down the dirt road, she would have set a brisk pace while I stayed as close to her as possible. This woman, who seemed to be afraid of nothing, had no idea how scared I was as I pictured bears and coyotes lurking in the darkness. Despite my racing heart, though, I was always aware of the sound of the peepers in the swamp near us. At that time, I didn't know that the singing was being done by the males calling to the females. I didn't know that the peeper got its technical name from the x-shaped cross on its back. I didn't even know that the one to one-and-a-half-inch creatures, which I have yet to see, should have been too small to make so much noise. All I knew was that theirs was a comforting sound to a seven-year-old who was trying not to think about the unnerving screech of an owl while avoiding stepping on her grandmother's heels.

In the years that have followed those walks of my childhood, the song of the peepers has mingled with other sounds at my grandparents': the whistle of the train that passed on the tracks behind their house en route to the paper mill in Millinocket, the clinking of the metal bowls of the milk separator as my grandmother cleaned them morning and night, the crowing of the rooster, which never fully woke me up.

That farm with its myriad sounds has long been gone, but the first peeping of the frogs always brings back memories of the countless days I spent there. Every year I say that I am going to preserve those memories by making a tape of their singing to cheer me on one of those bitter winter nights when the snow is deep and the wind is blowing and I can't even remember what warm feels like. Their music will remind me that soon the snow will melt, the days will become longer and the spring will return.

Let the poets praise the robin as the harbinger of the new season.
For me, the little frog with the big name will serve just as well.

Le Grand Ménage
By Bobbie Morrow

How delightful is the robin's cheerful spring song to ears that have
been bonneted, earmuffed, or otherwise covered during the long winter
months. When we were children, those happy tunes helped cure any
lingering "winteritus" we might have had and ushered in jump-rope-
jingle season, marble games during school recess time, and playing
hopscotch in the gravelly squares we drew in our driveway.

However, the melodies also evoked a new and restless energy
in Mom and Dad (Edwina Lefrancois Thibodeau and Fernand E.
Thibodeau), as well as in the other adults in our lives.

Mom developed a renewed interest in the kitchen cupboards,
which she completely emptied and thoroughly cleaned to a soft luster
before replacing or rearranging their contents. Our closets, next to
receive her attention, yielded mounds of assorted clothing laid out
across twin-sized beds, as well as sundry collections of "treasures" that
we had squirreled away months ago and then forgotten. Many a lively
game of make-believe, tag, or hide-and-go-seek had to be interrupted
when Mom needed us to try on last year's clothing, which she would
then alter, hand down to a smaller sister, or repurpose into colorful
quilts and fashionable outfits for our doll babies. We kids knew it was
getting to be that time again.

Meanwhile, Dad would arrive home from his day's work to enjoy
supper with the family, then with a vigorous "can-do" pep in his step
begin to make needed repairs to the house, do chores around the

yard, or clean the garage. Though patches of snow and ice stubbornly remained in shady spots near the rosebush and under the poplar tree, his push lawn mower suddenly emerged from hibernation, as did dusty garden tools and tight-lidded paint cans. Oh yes, it would be time soon.

When our grandmothers, aunts, or the neighbor ladies came to call, a certain topic was invariably discussed, and while stirring, sugaring, and sipping their coffees, they shared the lengthy litany of it, encouraging one another and dispensing time-tested advice. It seemed people mentioned this particular matter wherever we went, be it at church with the family, the post office to buy stamps with Mom, or even at the grocery store where shoppers' carts were likely to hold pine-scented cleaner, polish, floor wax, or powdered cleanser, as well as food stuffs.

And sure enough, we came home from school one day to be greeted by the sights, sounds, and smells of *le grand ménage*! It was time to do the BIG housekeeping, roughly translated from the French term. For the next few weeks we lived in a sort of orderly disorder as Mom did the *grand ménage* in our home. Like her own mother (Esther Thibodeau Lefrancois) and grandmother (Alice Ruest Thibodeau) before her, Mom espoused the idea that dust and dirt settle towards the lowest point, so began by cleaning the upstairs rooms first, methodically working her way downstairs. The furniture was moved out of the way and polished, ceilings and walls washed with hot, soapy water, and the floors scrubbed and waxed to a bright sheen. Nothing in the house was left untouched by soap, polish, or wax, and everything seemed shiny new again, fresh smelling and clean.

The practice of *le grand ménage* dates back to our French Acadian ancestors who, according to Anne Roy, director of the Acadian Village Historical Site in Van Buren, did *le grand ménage* in both spring and fall. Why in both seasons you might ask? The varied examples of Acadian artifacts and architecture found at the Acadian Village give us a wonderful glimpse into the past and help us to understand why this was so.

We learn that the earlier homes, constructed of square hewn logs, utilized a large, though inefficient, stone fireplace as a source of heat and for cooking. In later years, wood stoves served the same purposes. Roy explained that homemade tallow candles and kerosene lamps later on, added to the smoky atmosphere. This combined with cooking vapors and dust from the gardens and fields created a dingy residue all about the house, especially noticeable on the walls, which were often whitewashed.

Roy described the Acadian women as being meticulous in their cleaning habits. This trait is corroborated by Julie D. Albert, in *The Acadians of Maine*, where we read that French Acadian women had a reputation for keeping a clean house, so much so that the edges of the ceiling beams in some of their homes were worn round by scrubbing. These hard-working women passed the tradition of *le grand ménage* from one generation to the next, and so it was continued wherever the families settled, including the St. John Valley.

When the fall cleaning was completed, the women had time to weave, knit, create blankets and linens, as well as mend and make clothing before the cycle of planting, harvesting, and preserving of meats and foods began again.

My great-grandparents (Cyr and Alice Thibodeau) lived on a farm on the Canadian side of the St. John River where they grew their own food and raised their own animals, including sheep whose wool was hand-sheared each spring. Once the wool had been washed and carded, great-grandmother Alice would spin it into yarn with which she knitted stockings, hats, and other warm woolen articles. Mom fondly remembers helping her wind the creamy colored yarn. Great-grandmother Alice also wove blankets, made rag rugs, and sewed clothing for the family. Some of these fiber arts were passed along to Grandmother Esther Lefrancois. A talented seamstress, she also created much of her family's clothing and knitted countless pairs of socks and mittens for them and for all the grandchildren as they came along. Mom, also an accomplished seamstress, continued to sew, knit, and crochet many beautiful items, gifting the family and others with the work of her hands.

Though *le grand ménage* was primarily a woman's task, great-grandmother Alice enlisted the aid of great-grandfather, her sons, or the farmhand to move heavy wooden furniture and to bring bulky rugs outside to be beaten and cleaned. In their retirement years, before Dad's health failed, my parents partnered together to do some of *le grand ménage*. Dad's fine attention to detail made him a very good helper. With today's busy lifestyles and work schedules, many people now share household tasks and chores.

I recall my first experience participating in *le grand ménage* many years ago. Mom was going to teach me how to wash and wax my bedroom floor. Beginning in the far corner of the room, Mom showed me how to wet down about an arm's length section of the floor with hot water, sprinkle it evenly with cleanser, scrub it back and forth with the wooden brush to remove the old wax, and then how to carefully rinse it clean. It looked easy enough to me and as a young teenager with lots of things to do and places to go, I thought I'd be finished in no time by cleaning a larger area at a time with a more generous sprinkling of cleanser. With lots of splashing, sprinkling, scrubbing, and rinsing.

I moved quickly across the room until, to my consternation, I noticed that the floor was drying to a gritty, swirly white mess and had to be redone. It was not easy, took a lot of time, and though tired by the time the last coat of wax had dried, I was very proud of my floor's beautiful, glossy shine and took extra care to keep it looking as such. The value of a job well done, be it large or small, is often priceless. I continued to learn from Mom's wealth of experience and knowledge.

With the advent of modern appliances, clean-burning heat sources, and no-wax flooring—not to mention robot vacuum cleaners, "swiffer" dusters and erasers that make dirt and grime disappear—our cleaning needs and methods have changed. Some households even hire housekeepers or cleaning companies to do *le grand ménage* or other housecleaning tasks.

Although the French Acadian practice of *le grand ménage* is still *de rigueur* for some, today many of us, including myself, tend to such labor-intensive tasks whenever we find the time, and not necessarily in the spring or fall.

Now, what is that sweet sound I'm hearing outside my window? Oh, the robins are back! Can it be that time already?

The St. John River Valley
By Darrell McBreairty

The St. John River flows from Baker Pond to the Bay of Fundy past quiet towns on each side of the border where both French and English (Canadian and American) arrive to eke a living from the forests and the land. Generation after generation have passed on and are buried in tiny cemeteries not far from its bank, and the river continues—angry in the spring, calm and serene in summer and autumn, covered with ice in winter, with cold wind howling down its spine to the sea. Through generations it has stolen lives of men and boys, and flooded communities, and held up log drives, and destroyed boats and supplies—but the St. John is the force that created the Valley.

In the late eighteenth century, the Acadians came up the river away from the Loyalist settlers below Grand Falls, and then the descendants of those same Loyalists came in search of quick money and perhaps a place to live. Now the river's banks hold them all—living and dead, Catholic and Protestant, French and English, Canadian and American. At the end of the Bloodless Aroostook War, the St. John became the boundary between British Canada and the State of Maine, but governments do not make boundaries and neither does drawing lines on a map. For years, the people of the St. John Valley were one. The river tied them, and there was little desire to leave its banks and search out an easier existence.

The river had washed into their souls, and the land whispered to them in the night even when it lay frozen under mountains of snow. It was their Valley and after generations they became the Valley—a part of the river, and the land, and the sky that stretched over them, reaching out to the borders of a world they knew little of; but the world wars changed them and made them part of a national consciousness. The death of the lumber drives separated them. Now they are Americans and Canadians, although they are both part of the Valley where their ancestors had shared hardships and celebrations for generations. Now the river that had joined them, separates them into two nations, the way a handful of American radicals had planned at the beginning of the Bloodless Aroostook War.

Crossing the Border
By Jenny Radsma

Crossing the border was a new experience for me when I moved to Maine to live in a town that overlooked Canada, my home country. Previous to this move, I had rarely crossed the 49th parallel by car, but I soon came to discover the frequency with which people crossed, as they called it, and the norms that accompanied each crossing into Canada or back into the U.S.

For the first several weeks after my midwinter arrival, each time I made my way across the border, the customs and immigration officers would ask, "Where are you from?" I thought—mistakenly, I soon came to realize—I was being asked about my history, where I'd come from most recently, where my people were from, where did I call home? I would launch into how I had just come from Alberta, northern Alberta at that, that now I was living in Fort Kent, that I was going back to Alberta in June to pack all of my belongings at which time I would make a permanent move to Maine, and that, no, I did not own this car but was borrowing it from a friend who lived in New Brunswick, that it would not be part of the goods I'd be bringing with me when I returned to stay later that summer. I wondered if they wanted to know that my parents were Dutch immigrants who'd come to Calgary as part of the post-World War II flood of farmers and carpenters, mothers and fathers, who'd come to make a home for themselves and their children, and now here was I, one of those children, crossing into the United States to make a life for myself. I finally glanced at the border guard to see if he wanted any more details, and thought fleetingly he looked bored, his eyes glazed over in a way they hadn't been when he'd first signaled me to approach the window.

When I finally stopped talking, he'd say, "Anything to declare?" which was also foreign to me. Declare? What was I to declare? That I was a Canadian? That my parents had been born in Holland? That I had four sisters? I caught on, though, that "no" was expected, the typical answer savvy people gave when crossing the border so they could be motioned to move on. In this way, crossing the border should only have taken about ten to twenty seconds but, initially, took me mental rehearsal, great angst, and several minutes to tell my story to the customs and immigration personnel on either side of the border. In time, I came to learn they had no interest in my lineage or that I was about to visit the daughter of a friend who still lived in Alberta but who would be moving back to New Brunswick later in the summer, at the same time as I.

Eventually I came to understand that when crossing the border, brevity was expected: answer only what is asked.

"Where are you headed?"

"Harvey Station."

"What's your citizenship?"

"Canadian."

"What's your status in the U.S.?"

"I'm on a visa."

"Do you have any guns, ammunition, mace, or pepper spray with you?"

"No."

"Do you have any alcohol or tobacco with you?"

"No."

"What's the value of any goods you may be leaving behind in Canada?"

"Twenty dollars U.S."

"What's the nature of your visit?"

"Social."

"How long do you plan to stay in Canada?"

"Two nights."

"Have a good day, ma'am."

That was for crossing into Canada. Heading back into the U.S. wasn't much better, as I then had to show my visa and give my litany to customs officers who at the same time were peering into my car and rummaging about in my trunk to see if any contraband could be found among the almost empty jug of wiper fluid, maps, umbrella, bungee cords, and windshield scrapers. Slow as I was to this new pastime of border crossing, I caught on and learned to charm. Now, each time I crossed, my goal was to engage with the "guys" to see how little I would get asked. Mind you, this became much easier to do after I had my own car with Maine license plates, not an old rusted Toyota Corolla with New Brunswick plates, registered in someone else's name, that didn't meet American EPA standards.

It was also easier to do in Fort Kent, where the men and women, who protected the northern border of their country from ne'er-do-wells and would-be terrorists, came to recognize and know me. Indeed, a friend and I drove across the border with such regularity, that one guard came to refer to us as Thelma and Louise. "Well, if it isn't Thelma and Louise out again tonight!" he'd say, a friendly grin on his face. And despite that it was post-9/11, with entry into the U.S. typically characterized by vigilant and less-than-friendly border personnel, on those occasions when I crossed the border alone, without my friend, he'd ask me where Louise was. I guess that made me Thelma.

Good Neighbors
By Ron Laing

In 1914, poet Robert Frost published his now famous poem "Mending Wall," in which he concludes: "Good fences make good neighbors." Maybe he's right.

In the little Aroostook town where I grew up, there was a road about two miles long, which went from the village of Westfield to U.S. Route 1, a highway that starts in Fort Kent, and ends in Key West, Florida.

I'm not sure this short connecting road had a name when I was a kid. Everyone just called it "The Road to the Corner." At some point the road was given a name, and they called it "Burleigh Road."

It just so happened that on this road, and not far out of the village, lived two uncles of mine. Their homes were side-by-side, with only a wooden fence separating the properties.

One uncle was Glenn Day, my mother's brother. The other uncle was Dad's brother, Russell Laing, and the two families were good neighbors and had lived in this close proximity for several years. Each family rented the house they lived in.

When I was a child, I often visited my uncles, and regardless of which one I came to call on that day, I almost always spent time with the other family, too.

The time came when Russell made an offer to purchase a home, and it just happened to be the one Glenn was living in. Glenn, however, was unaware his lesser-valued house was for sale.

After the deal was complete, Russell informed his neighbor of his purchase. Of course, Glenn was surprised, and now must find another home for his family. He reluctantly told his wife, Jennie, the bad news. Only six months earlier she had given birth to their first child, Garland. Together they pondered where they might live.

That very evening the little family had been invited to supper at Glenn's parents' farm on the Egypt Road. After the meal they mentioned they were looking for a new home.

"Don't you like the house you're in?" Glenn's dad asked.

"Oh, we do—but Russell informed us he has bought that property and plans to live there himself."

"That's strange, for the house he's living in is a much better home than the one you're in," Grandfather Day remarked.

"I know it is—but it's something they can afford, I guess. They may find it too small for their family because it's too small for us, and they have more kids."

"Let me think about this," Grandfather said, and everyone wondered what he was up to.

The next afternoon my grandfather stopped to see his old friend, the one who just happened to own the house Russell was renting.

"Ever think of selling that house after Russell moves out?" Grandfather asked.

"Well—I didn't expect Russell to be leaving so soon. I've not given it a lot of thought, Tracy."

"If you were of a mind to sell, maybe I'd be of a mind to buy."

When Grandfather drove his old Dodge from his friend's yard, he was the new owner of a house on "The Road to the Corner."

After papers were drawn up and signed, Grandfather told Glenn of his acquisition and gave him first chance should he want to rent. He also said he'd work out a purchase plan if they wished to buy, and within a day the young couple decided they wanted to purchase.

The weekend came and Russell noticed Glenn busy in his yard. "When are you moving?" he said, coming close to the fence.

"Very soon. Last week we bought a place, and as soon as the people living in that house move, we'll be out of here."

"I sure hope it's soon!" said Russell and walked away not completely satisfied.

"Where'd you find a house, anyway?" Russell called over his shoulder.

"Oh, right here in town. It's a nice home, too. Better than this one, and a place I've wanted for a long time."

"Well, tell the guy who lives there to hurry and move, will you?" said Russell.

"I will," Glenn replied. "And Russell, by the way I think you should move soon." Russell looked puzzled.

A week went by before the two met again.

"Hate to force you, old boy, but I've got to get into my new house. You've got to move so I can get in there!" Russell was provoked.

"The sooner you get out, the sooner I'll be moving in," said Glenn.

"That makes no sense at all, Glenn," Russell replied, as a puzzled look crossed his face.

"You're the one holding things up, Russell."

"Me?"

"Yes, you! The house I bought is the house you're leaving. Hasn't your landlord told you?"

"He hasn't." Russell kicked the ground in disgust. "You've been messing with me, Glenn, haven't you?"

"Not at all. Well—a little maybe."

The following weekend a section of the wooden fence came down and the two families moved their belongings into each other's homes. At age 5, I was not old enough to be of much help, but old enough to be in the way.

"Just stay out of the way, and don't ask so many questions!" both uncles told me.

I spent the whole day watching a funny sight. All day long the two families moved stuff from one house to the next, each helping the other move things, especially the heavy furniture.

I thought perhaps the old fence might not go back up, but it did. For the next twenty-some years these two families lived side-by-side and were friends.

Maybe Frost was right! Good fences do make good neighbors.

My Father's Pine Boxes

By Torrey Sylvester

I can recall Dad saying for years after I got out of the Navy in 1965 that when he "shuffled off this mortal coil" he wanted to be buried in Mars Hill where he was born and where his grandparents are buried in Pierce Cemetery on the Fort Fairfield Road.

When a friend of Dad's was remodeling the old Fair Street Grammar School in Houlton, Dad asked the carpenter, Joe Girvan, to save him some of the wide pine boards, planks really, in the school. "Why?" Joe asked.

"Because I want you to build two boxes (coffins) for my wife and me!" Dad said. Joe was stunned.

"Why," he asked, "do you want them now? You're not old enough or even sick." Dad was firm as he laughed, "I just want to be ready when the day comes." Joe shrugged and agreed.

Some weeks later he arrived at Dad's place in New Limerick and backed up to the barn. In the back of his pickup were two solid pine plank coffins, one six feet long and the other one about five foot three inches—my mother's height. She even lay down in it to see if she fit! That made everyone laugh. Dad approved of the craftsmanship and he and Joe stored them in a back corner of the barn for future use. Joe laughed and shook his head as Dad paid him the thirty dollars Joe wanted. Dad tried to give him more, but Joe wouldn't hear of it.

In the following months and years many of Dad's friends heard of his "boxes" and came to the barn to see them. Their reactions amused Dad, ranging from simple curiosity to near revulsion at the macabre nature of the talk. One golfing buddy of Dad's asked why on earth he would do that at any time much less now when he wasn't even sick? Dad replied, "Good question—'cause I want to be planted in the earth I came from in Mars Hill." Dad mused how many folks wouldn't discuss their deaths; it scared them I guess. Not Dad. He embraced the discussion and preparation for his death.

The years rolled by from 1960 when the pine boxes were built. In 1970, the unexpected happened and Dad got lung cancer from his years of smoking Lucky Strikes and Camels, unfiltered of course. The cancer spread and by the fall of 1973 he was really sick, so my family and I moved back to the Houlton area from Bangor. In that year I had many opportunities to discuss the plans for his funeral with him. He was firm, no funeral service. Just put him in his box and "plant him" beside his grandparents in Mars Hill.

Dad asked me repeatedly if I would do as he asked and I assured him our family would. Time dragged on as he got worse. Finally the winter passed and spring arrived in The County. Dad's sixty-sixth birthday, May 18, approached but it was clear he wasn't going to make

it. He had been home for the last year, going out only for his radia-
tion and chemotherapy treatments. He loved sunshine and would sit
or lie on the rug in his south facing living room across from the golf
course in New Limerick. He had only been retired two years after
twenty-eight years at F.A. Peabody Company.

Friends would visit, talk and reminisce with him about old times,
especially sports. Dad loved sports of all kinds, but golf and basketball
were his favorites. He played basketball at Aroostook Central Institute
in Mars Hill and the University of Maine where he was captain of the
varsity team his senior year, 1930. He picked up golf in his forties and
was playing bogey golf in no time to the consternation of his cronies.

Dad remained mentally alert through his last days even though his
body was failing him. Finally the end of his life was clearly near and
the last four days he was so sick that Mom couldn't care for him so he
was admitted to the Aroostook General Hospital in Houlton. Monday
noon, April 29, 1974, he drew his last deep shuddering breath and life
left his body. We who lived near were all present to say our goodbyes.

The nurses helped us wrap him in his winding sheet. We placed
his body on a gurney and took him down in the elevator to my station
wagon. I distinctly remember a nurse on the elevator saying, "Can
you do this?" Well, we could and we did. It was what Dad wanted,
a loving family "hands on" experience to ease his body into its final
resting place.

We took him the five miles to his beloved barn at "High Hopes"
in New Limerick and gently placed him in his pine box in his old red
bathrobe that my mother had made for him. We added mementos
and before we nailed the "pine box" shut, Mom gently removed his
wedding band and put it on her middle finger. Then we carried the
box with its precious cargo into the kitchen and placed it in the spring
sunshine that was streaming in the windows.

My mother placed a beautiful old handmade family heirloom
quilt over the pine box and Dad's portrait sat on top. I remember my

young daughter, then only five years old, sitting on the box and asking where Grampy's head was. My mother kneeled down beside her, they figured it out and we all laughed and cried together.

Many friends and neighbors, hearing of the death of Fred A. Sylvester Jr., "Slim," came to the house to pay their respects until late that evening. Most accepted Dad's independent streak and his wishes but some questions still were asked. We simply said this is what he wanted —an old-fashioned farm family funeral. His requests were fulfilled and he was in his pine box at last at the young age of sixty-five plus.

The next day, Tuesday, we placed the pine box in my station wagon and headed slowly to Mars Hill. By noon we had arrived with a caravan of cars behind us, and the grave next to his grandparents in Pierce Cemetery was opened. We lowered his pine box gently down, our pastor said the 23rd Psalm, we sang some hymns, then threw dirt on the box. We laughed and cried and asked ourselves, "How did we just do this?" We were at once in awe of what had just happened and surprised that it was so perfectly easy and right.

The important thing was we did just exactly what he wanted, his cycle was complete and he was "planted" in his pine box. Mom's comment was that she knew where her box was when her time came. She had to wait thirty-five more years to use her "pine box" but that's another story.

Finding the Cedar Spring
By Cherry B. Danker

Nestled at the base of the grove of cedar trees, in a mossy swamp of the old farm's far southwest corner, a cedar spring lay waiting. Back in the 1920s, my father rocked it up and for years it served as an additional source of water when the fields were dry. My father always said its drinking water was the best in the whole, wide world. I believed him. My earliest memory of drinking from the cedar spring was with him. A communal tin dipper hung from the top of a sturdy stick at the outer edge of the spring. My father would fill the dipper with the clear, cold water, and he would drink with gusto. When he finished he filled the dipper again and presented it to me with a flourish.

"Nectar from the gods," he always proclaimed. I, too, would drink, aping my father. I agreed that we were sampling a bit of the heavens.

Throughout my childhood and into my teens, the cedar spring was my special place of magic power. On the long, hot days of summer, I wandered there when I was lonely, hurt, or sad. I would take a book, an old lounging blanket that was once my Aunt Myrtie's carriage lap robe, and a lunch of an apple, cheese, and crackers. My walk down back on the farm road took me into the fresh, cool embrace of the forest. At the cedar spring, I dreamed of the far-off places I would go when I got big.

My father died in 1965 several years after he stopped farming. The farm evolved into an abundance of low, woody, perennial plant life which served as underbrush for a new growth of fast rising trees. The farm road that led down back to the cedar spring faded into oblivion. After several failed attempts to locate it, the family thought the cedar spring was lost and gone forever. I was unwilling to accept the loss of the cedar spring. After I retired from my job in Washington, D.C., and settled in Portage, not far from the old farm, I often ventured, alone, down through the unfamiliar terrain of dense thicket. I, too, failed to find my special place of magic power.

In the summer of 1991, a severe drought plagued northern Maine. The cistern went dry in the old farmhouse. My brother, Nelson, thought the well also might go dry, and he resolved to find the rocked-up, cedar spring. He remembered to watch for the grove of cedar trees in that far, southwest corner. On his third try, he led my mother, my sister, and me right to it. The tall cedars waved gently in the breeze as we walked in and the spring gurgled a sweet welcome. We were amazed to find it as well rocked up as when we last saw it. Kneeling, we peered into its mysterious depths, and we saw and heard the bubbles. Making cups of our hands, we drank with gusto.

"Nectar from the gods," my mother proclaimed, and we laughed with warm nostalgia. Nelson planted a sturdy new stick on which to hang a communal dipper. Back at the farmhouse, I prowled through trunks in the attic and retrieved the carriage lap robe. On future long, hot summer days, when I am lonely, hurt, or sad, I will take the robe, a book, and a lunch of an apple, cheese and crackers, and walk back down through the thicket to the rocked-up cedar spring.

The Wellspring
By Gordon Hammond

It was the year Brooks Robinson played third base like a Hoover and the Big Red Machine ground to a halt in Baltimore Memorial Stadium. I was on a weekend retreat in the White Mountains. We'd just completed a game of tennis and were walking it off in the cool shade of a country road. It was very quiet.

Ears accustomed to city sounds sifted through the low humming of the summer afternoon and rested on a soft rushing sound in the woods. In the heat of the day we were drawn to the coolness and found a small stream winding down the mountain and under the road.

I lived and worked in Boston. Clear mountain streams weren't a big part of my life, but the sight of the clear water brought back a memory from long ago—that of a ten-year-old boy lying in the grass of a meadow drinking cold water from a spring-fed pool. Now, twenty-three years and uncountable glasses of chlorinated water later, I was down again, belly first on a flat rock, thrusting my sweat-streaked face into that sparkling stream.

When a seed is planted it can take time to sprout. For me, that moment in the mountains started a process that eventually saw me walk away from a career—all because of a drink of cold water on a hot summer day.

When I arrived in Aroostook County in June 1975 to explore a piece of land in Westfield, I had an opportunity to repeat the experience. Just a few yards into the woods from an abandoned field, I found a small stream slipping almost unnoticed through a moss and jewelweed woodland. And there again was a flat rock just waiting for a warm belly. The stream began deep in the woods in a remote area so there was little danger of contamination from farm chemicals. I lay down and drank. The coolness washed away the years and I saw the man on the mountainside and the boy in the meadow and the seed sent its shoot skyward through the yielding earth.

I bought the land—or rather the stream and the land attached to it and the trees that kept the stream cool in the summer heat. That fall I moved from Massachusetts to The County.

I didn't move to Maine, you understand, I moved to Aroostook County. There is a difference. I felt a need for life essentials that were missing. I had great hopes of finding them here in these fields and woods and by this stream. That, in Aroostook, I could draw a deep breath without encroaching on my neighbor's air supply was one consideration, but there was more.

Beginning at the Sumner Tunnel in Boston and moving northward through Exxon stations and Howard Johnsons, I noticed a dramatic change in the people. They were more pleasant and more calm, but mostly, they looked at me! Not through, by, or around me, but at me. I responded gratefully, and by the time I reached Sherman, the temperature, humidity, and my blood pressure were dueling to see which could reach the most accommodating level.

I was apprehensive about going into the wilds of the north, but with each new experience I began to realize that my concerns were based on a lack of information. Back in Boston, Caribou seemed a stretch of tundra just northeast of Hudson's Bay and Aroostook County had a sound that seemed muffled by old burlap bags. I was amazed to find that I could board a plane in Boston and land in a place called Presque Isle in much the same way I traveled in the other direction to LaGuardia. And the plane *even* returned from Presque Isle and more than once a month! In retrospect, those comments are still amusing, but now they're meaningful. They make a point—Aroostook County is a secret.

But it's a secret with some benefits. The limited awareness of a region where people live, work, and play has helped maintain the stability and purity of its character. Aroostook County has yet to be homogenized. The spirit of cooperation, of independence, of family and community are all around us here. The hype hasn't penetrated the green and blue barrier that protects the strong value system that preserved this region for so long; that created an environment that is at once rare and reassuring.

People will come, as I did, and may stumble on a wellspring near a meadow on the edge of the woods and feel alive to all the possibilities (the mind goes free here and there are no real limits.) Some drink their fill and return to the "reality" of the world south, not willing or able to break the cord. But whether we stay or go, once we've been, we're never the same again.

The Year with No Summer

By Merle Tyrrell

Volcanic eruptions were far down on the list of things to worry about when the first settlers from southern New England arrived in what was to become Houlton in 1807. Nevertheless, one far-off eruption was to inflict unnatural hardship on their frontier enterprise.

The initial surveying party of pioneers from New Salem, Massachusetts, made the trip by canoe up the Penobscot and Mattawamkeag rivers, through the Grand Lake system east of Danforth into New Brunswick, down the Eel River to Meductic, up the St. John River to the already thriving town of Woodstock, and then twelve miles through the woods to their homestead sites in Maine. Subsequent immigrants generally took a more indirect, but much less exhausting route by sea to Fredericton via Saint John and then up the river by towboat to Woodstock, which had been founded some years earlier by refugee Tories and Loyalist militia following their defeat in the American Revolution. Woodstock played a major supporting role in the settlement of the southern Aroostook area. When the newly independent United States again went to war with the British Empire in 1812, residents of Woodstock and Houlton agreed that if there were to be war it had best be waged by others in some other place; the northern wilderness was big enough for both sides.

The forest was full of game and the waters were alive with fish. As long as sunshine warmed the fertile soil and rain came to nourish their early crops, the self-reliant Houlton folk were little concerned with what went on outside. But in 1816, just nine years after the founding of the town, the unthinkable happened. Following a particularly severe winter, the promise of spring was not fulfilled. Instead of the expected warm sunshine, there was heavy frost in May and June, and again in July and August. Instead of life-renewing rain there was ice and snow, as much as nine inches of it in northern Aroostook in June. And it was all because of something that had happened half a world away.

The Aroostook pioneers didn't know about it until long after having endured its effect, but in April 1815, Mount Tambora, on the island of Sumbawa, south of Borneo in what is now Indonesia, erupted, spewing thirty-eight cubic miles of debris into the atmosphere. Most of it came right back down again, raining death and destruction on Sumbawa and its neighbors. But a vast cloud of fine dust particles remained in the atmosphere to diffuse the sun's light and create (in the following year) the coldest summer ever recorded in much of the Northern Hemisphere.

The dust cloud from the volcano was not recognized in Houlton or anywhere else as the cause of the strange, frigid summer. Some blamed it on that year's unusual sunspots, which were visible to the naked eye at sunrise and sunset. Others proclaimed both the sunspots and the weather to be portents of the approaching end of the world. In one of the first apocalyptic warnings about the dangers of perverse tinkering with nature, a scholar at the Milan Observatory in Italy claimed the cold weather was due to the increasing proliferation of Ben Franklin's lightning rods, already under attack as vain attempts to thwart the vengeful purposes of the Almighty. The devilish devices were supposedly sucking the mysterious element "electricity" out of the atmosphere and storing it in the ground. Or they were drawing it out of the ground and spewing it into the atmosphere; the record isn't clear, but either way it had to be stopped.

All of New England, in a year that came to be known as "Eighteen Hundred and Froze to Death," suffered from the freakish weather. There was, in fact, a report of a man having frozen to death in New Hampshire in June. He became lost while out searching for his cows in a storm. His body was found in the snow the next morning, cold and stiff. There was no autopsy or coroner's report and it's likely he had suffered a heart attack. But "froze to death in June" made a better story, although it would not do for Aroostook—No resident of "The County" then or now would ever speak of freezing to death at any temperature above forty below.

At Houlton, the summer-long frost killed all grain crops except rye, the hardiest, and that was scant and of poor quality. There was little bread to eat until after the harvest the following year. A few root crops planted in high ground survived, but even a good crop would not have made up for the loss of wheat, oats, and corn. Livestock fodder was a major concern and the little hay harvested had to be carefully rationed the following winter. Cows foraged in the woods during the summer and continued to produce two pails of milk each day, which could be made into one pound of butter. New milk changed to curd and mixed with cream and maple sugar was "nutritious and palatable—a good substitute for custard," according to a history of the period recorded in the July 13, 1857 edition of the *Aroostook Pioneer* and reprinted in the August 15, 1957, edition of the *Houlton Pioneer Times.*

By the fall of 1816 grain from the southern United States was beginning to arrive in Saint John and Fredericton, but at prices beyond the reach of most. Rye flour became available at seventeen dollars a barrel in Woodstock at a time when a thousand board feet of sawn lumber delivered there fetched a mere ten or twelve dollars. The same relative comparison today would make the cost of the flour nearly three hundred dollars. Few Houlton folks had that kind of money, but with no crops to tend they had plenty of time to cut and saw logs. Many turned to making hand-split cedar shingles, which required little equipment to produce. Lashed together into rafts they could be floated to Woodstock on the Meduxnekeag River, which runs through Houlton, and exchanged there for provisions. But that delivery method wasn't quite as straightforward as it sounds.

About ten miles downriver, at a place called Jackson Falls, the Meduxnekeag tumbles down a long series of rock-strewn cataracts. Rafters had to put ashore, carry their shingles bundle by bundle around the falls, and then reassemble the raft in the gorge below. One such trip is described in the 1858 *Aroostook Pioneer*.

In November of 1816 when the river was in full flood after the fall rains, a "young man and a boy of some years" set out with a raft of shingles for Woodstock. Apparently lacking in experience, they barely avoided being swept over the falls, but did succeed in putting ashore at the last possible moment. They hand-carried the shingles through the woods a distance of three hundred yards to a point where they thought they could safely rebuild the raft and continue on to Woodstock. They didn't get far before they ran onto a sandbar where the raft broke up and the shingles floated free. Some went downriver, but most were lost to the bushes and backwaters. The two novice river drivers survived their dunking in the icy water, salvaged their tools and provisions, and made a raft of long cedar logs on which they drifted another ten or twelve miles to Woodstock.

After drying out overnight they procured a birch bark canoe and started poling and paddling back upriver to retrieve their payload. Soaking wet again from having capsized twice more on the way, the exhausted pair managed to reach the falls where they found a man camped ashore beside a roaring fire. They spent the night beating a path around and around the fire, the water in their clothing slowly turning to steam, which drifted away in the cold November air. The next morning, they reassembled their raft bit by bit as they drifted down to Woodstock. There they marketed their shingles and used the money to buy scarce food items and other supplies which they tied up in blankets and carried on their backs twelve miles overland to Houlton.

Back home, according to the 1858 report, they "told the sad story [in the tavern] which, though pitiful, yet extorted laughter from the facetious guests, listening to the rehearsal of the duckings they had, their desperate swimming effort in the freezing elements . . . [the listeners] exclaimed, 'Such fellows were not reared in the woods to be frightened by an owl or a quail before a storm!'"

Friendly Village
By Sandy Lynch

The first time I flew into the airport in Presque Isle it was in the middle of a thunderstorm. The year was 1968 and I was 17. I should have been scared, but instead I felt guilty. My father had a lifelong love of airplanes and should have been the first one in our family to ride in an airplane. Instead, that afternoon he stood on the observation deck at LaGuardia Airport in New York City and waved as I lifted off into the sky in a Northeast Airlines Yellowbird.

I was too excited to feel guilty for long. I was on my way to the Potato Blossom Festival in a town I didn't even know existed until I met Jerry Lynch, a plebe midshipman at the United States Merchant Marine Academy in Kings Point, Long Island. I had gone there with some friends from church for a mixer. He asked me to dance, but for most of the evening we talked about his friends from high school, his family, and Fort Fairfield, the town where he grew up. He left for the academy orientation in July right after his high school graduation when all of his friends were getting ready for one last summer of fun before attending the University of Maine. It was October but it was obvious he was still homesick. I was sympathetic, but like most of my friends at the time, I had a true New Yorker's myopic view of the world. I believed, as John Updike wrote, "People living anywhere else had to be, in some sense, kidding."

After that we had many dates and he filled me in with more and more details about life in that small town. He told me about growing up on White Hill Street in a house on a street of homes that his father had built. His father owned a construction company and the only hardware store in town, C. J. Lynch Co. It was clear that he was homesick for his family and his five brothers and sisters but also for the familiar surroundings of Fort Fairfield. He talked about playing trumpet in the high school band and marching in the Potato Blossom Festival parade. We looked through his yearbook and he read me excerpts from *The Fort Fairfield Review* and the Tom E. Rott column filled with local gossip. He described picking potatoes and how all the schools had time off in the fall to allow the students to help with the harvest. He talked about the cold winters and the mountains of snow that they walked through on the way to school.

Going to school in New York public schools I had experienced a very different reality. There were few days off from school due to weather and any snow that fell quickly turned to ankle-deep gray slush. There were so many students in my high school that we had to have two separate sessions to accommodate everyone. The fact that potatoes had blossoms was a revelation, too. I came from a meat and potatoes family, but I don't think I ever gave a thought to where potatoes came from or how they grew.

As the plane descended onto the runway and slowly taxied to a stop, I was surprised to see fields of pink flowers on either side of the runway and a farmer on his tractor driving parallel to the plane. The terminal was a small building packed with people waiting to greet relatives and servicemen returning to Loring Air Force Base. It was the height of the Vietnam War and the Presque Isle Airport was a busy place. It didn't take me long to find Jerry, though. He was wearing his Kings Point windbreaker. We gathered up my luggage and drove off in his Chevy Impala. The radio station was playing "Hey Jude" by the Beatles and listening to the familiar song, I started to relax.

It wasn't long before we were driving past fields and farms and structures that Jerry pointed out as potato houses. I was impressed that he could tell me what was growing in the fields just by looking at them. As we drove into the town of Fort Fairfield, we took a detour down Main Street. Jerry drove slowly, raising his hand off the steering wheel as cars passed in the other direction. When I asked him why he was doing that he said he was saying 'Hi' to people he knew. It seemed like he knew the driver in every car on Main Street! We drove past all the stores, the library, Northern National Bank, the drug store, the Plymouth Hotel, Ayoob Brothers Clothing Store, Ayoob's Smoke Shop, Sears, Achorn's, Goodhue Jewelers and all the way down to the Boundary Line Drive-in, until finally we turned back to C. J. Lynch's Trustworthy Hardware Store.

I didn't know what to expect. This was the 1960s—before Home Depot and Lowe's big box stores. At the time, I don't think I had ever been in a hardware store in the city. The building itself was old with lawn mowers and rakes displayed outside and kitchen wares in the large storefront windows. Jerry's mother, Rollande, was behind the cash register and his father, Clarence, came out from the back office to meet me. I shook hands with him, and I was surprised when he extended his left hand in a very strong handshake. It was only then that I realized his right arm hung motionless at his side. Jerry had described his father's accomplishments to me. He had been a champion baseball player and skier, but he never mentioned that his father had suffered from childhood polio. It was clear that neither he nor anyone else considered it a handicap.

Walking around in the store was like taking a step back in time. Jerry showed me the wall of wooden drawers each filled with a different type of screw, nail or washer. There were plumbing supplies, roofing supplies, shovels, paint, wallpaper, fishing gear, baking pans, canning supplies—in a small town it was one-stop shopping. Jerry hopped up to sit on the counter as I looked around. There were things I had never seen before—bean pots, potato baskets, hand-crank ice cream makers, and lobster steamers, just to name a few.

What really caught my eye was a full set of stoneware china dishes. Every dinner plate had a different country scene. In addition, there were all sorts of serving pieces—a turkey platter, pepper and salt shakers, a soup tureen, covered vegetable bowls, sugar and creamer, coffee pot, and teapot each with a different pastoral scene. I had never seen anything like it. I flipped over one of the plates to remember the manufacturer since I might never get back to this hardware store again. The set was called "Friendly Village" by Johnson Brothers. I made a mental note of it thinking that if and when I got married, I would love to have a set just like it.

Jerry asked me if I wanted to see what was on the floors above the store and I said, "Sure." He took me over to the wooden freight elevator that was unlike anything I had ever seen. I had taken the elevator to the top of the Empire State Building, but that was far less scary than inching up to the second floor of C.J. Lynch's Hardware store! The upper floor was filled with snow shovels, snow scoops, skidoos and snowshoes, and all kinds of winter equipment and stacks of paint cans.

The next day we were back at the store again. Main Street was filled with people and cars and the excitement was building for the start of the Potato Blossom Festival parade. The night before we had been to a street dance near the Post Office. I was glad I left my Twiggy-inspired false eyelashes at home. The girls who called out "Hi Jerome!" to Jerry weren't wearing a lot of makeup and looked as pretty as the Breck shampoo girls in the magazines. There were no "go-go" boots or mini-skirts and I felt a little overdressed, with my stockings and heels. It was a lot of fun though.

Jerry took me up to one of the apartments over the hardware store where we could get a bird's-eye view of the parade. I couldn't help feeling privileged to have such a good view—almost like the people I'd seen looking down from their penthouse windows when I watched the Macy's Thanksgiving Day Parade from the street on Central Park West in New York City. The Potato Blossom Festival parade was everything a parade should be—floats, beauty queens, marching bands, clowns and more huge tractors, combines, harvesters and farm equipment than I had ever seen in my life!

I tried to take as many photos as I could and remember everything to write in my diary when I returned home. Jerry was leaving for his "sea year" when he went back to the academy and I might not see him again. I remember thinking I probably would never get back to Fort Fairfield again either.

As it turned out, I did see Jerry again and I have been back to Fort Fairfield many times over the years. As a wedding present, we received a full set of "Friendly Village" china for twelve with all the serving pieces. The C.J. Lynch Hardware Store isn't there anymore and C.J. Lynch himself is gone, but every time we return for a family event or the Potato Blossom Festival and we pass the sign that reads "Welcome to Friendly Fort Fairfield!" I think of my first visit to Fort Fairfield almost fifty years ago and that "Friendly Village" china in C.J. Lynch's Hardware Store.

What Depression?

By Dorothy Boone Kidney

When my sister Kay and I were children, we were just poor enough to be rich. All year we cut out paper dolls from the Sears Roebuck catalogue. At Christmas, along with other gifts, we usually received a book of real paper dolls with cut-out clothes. Our appreciation and delight at Christmas were much greater because of our year-long experience of cutting out our own dolls from the catalogue.

Ice cream in those days was not any everyday affair, but an occasional Saturday night treat when Dad bought us each a small, chocolate-covered Eskimo pie (ten cents apiece—an astronomical price in those days) at Marston's Ice Cream Parlor. The long wait during the week made the ice cream taste much better.

We were blessed with loving, thrifty parents whose Saturday night and Christmas timing of small, inexpensive gifts was remarkable.

If Kay and I were poor during those Depression Days, we were not aware of it. Besides, everyone we knew in Presque Isle was in the same boat—so it certainly was a big boat!

And we were content. Some years we wore our shabby coats until Christmas, then excitedly tore Christmas paper off brand new coats. It never occurred to us that the coats were necessities held off until Christmas to look like luxuries.

Contentment was composed of a bright blue sweater, knit by our mother, and crisp red apples brought up from the cellar by our father to eat with the corn popped in the wire popper over the wood-burning kitchen range on winter evenings. We ate chicken just at Thanksgiving and Christmas in those days—ham was reserved for Easter. And we had watermelon just once a year on the Fourth of July. Those foods for us were holiday highlights. And, in between, we were happily contented with beef pies, baked beans, yeast rolls, garden vegetables, and homemade preserves.

I thought about all that the other day in the supermarket when I was purchasing chicken (not for Thanksgiving, but for an ordinary weekday meal), trying to decide which flavor of ice cream to buy and listening to a child fighting with his mother because he wanted all the toys on the shelf and all the candy in the store. I thought about it again when the television commercials blared at me urging me to buy a new car, to change my brand of shampoo, deodorant and detergent, to paint my house, and to buy a sofa.

I began to wonder what had happened to contentment. Had it gone out with the Great Depression? I recalled a verse from the Bible which admonishes: "Let your conversation be without covetousness; and be content with such things as ye have." (Hebrews 13:5)

Surrounded by daily temptations to purchase bigger and better things; coaxed constantly by television to change my lifestyle, and to trade in my old car for a newer model, contentment is not easy to come by. But there's peace and contentment in being satisfied with what you can afford.

And there is happiness in little things and small pleasures. I know. Yes, Kay and I were rich back in those days.

This House was Built on Honor
By Kathryn Olmstead

"I believe I was the only child at the inauguration of President Theodore Roosevelt. I was ten years old. We sat at the President's right during the parade and one of the things that caught my eye was Geronimo. He rode a pony in the parade and his headdress hung all the way to the ground. I believe it was one of his last public appearances.

"The next day we went to the Smithsonian and he was sitting on a settee out in front and I said, 'Oh, I'd like to speak to him.' I was so tickled to see him, I don't know what I said, but he just kind of grunted. He acted friendly, but he didn't try to say anything. And when I shook his hand it was so, so soft. It was just like a soft glove."

The speaker is Nancy Sewall Cunningham. She is seated with her husband, Maurice, in the living room of her family home in the center of Island Falls, just beneath the room where she was born ninety-four years ago. Her recollections of life in that house and of her parents' experiences before she was born are a mural of United States history that portrays the founding of a settlement, the coming of the railroad, the building of the tannery, and a constant flow of visitors—from rough woods workers to a man who would be President of the United States.

"They say my father was the first white baby born in Island Falls. They mean he was the first non-Indian. An Indian baby was born here the same day he was. They called him Pielle Sousop. He and my father played together."

Born April 13, 1845, William Wingate Sewall was the son of Island Falls' first white settlers. His pioneer parents, Levi and Rebecca Alexander Sewall, traveled to Island Falls after the factory where Levi worked as a shoemaker in Phippsburg, Maine, burned, leaving him "with quite a large family and nothing else," William told his daughter, Harriet Harmon in 1926.

"The reason why (Island Falls) was so called is very evident to anyone who has ever known the place," Sewall said. "There is an island in the center of the river with falls on either side. By nature it was endowed with beauty, though man has done much to destroy its natural charm. Tall pines grew on the island and the banks were clothed with wild flowers."

Levi resolved to find this spot after it was described to him by a friend. He and two friends found their way to Patten, and walked east through unbroken wilderness, "not knowing whether they were above the falls or below it" when they settled down to camp for the night.

"My father was always an early riser and in the profound stillness of the woods in the early morning could hear the sound of the falls," Sewall said. Accordingly, the party started toward it, and trees were felled for the log cabin that would be the birthplace of William.

Nancy Sewall Cunningham recalls her father with the same clarity and respect that he described his father.

"My father had a great eye for nature. He loved all the flowers and he taught me. He'd come in from the hayfield with blue-eyed grass stuck in his hatband for me. Once in a while he'd find a trailing arbutus . . . a ram's head lady's slipper . . . a little tiny orchid.

"His Aunt Sarah taught him and he taught me. He was under her care after he had diphtheria. They would go for long walks on pleasant Sundays up to the river. They'd sit down and she would teach him about nature. Then about sunset the wolves would start and that was a sign to pick up William and go home; that was like a bell. She'd say 'Come William. The wolves are calling. Time to go home.'

"He told us about the Indians who used to come down the river and camp near here seasonally. He described how they could take their canoes over the falls sideways by turning them broadside just so. He always spoke highly of the Indian and somehow we knew he felt that it had been hard for them as they were pushed back and back."

Seated before her living room hearth, Nancy takes me into her childhood, just as her father took her into his. We imagine a little girl, watching the people come and go in the big, white frame house that her grandfather and father built between 1865 and 1870, a house that hosted town meetings and was the town's first post office, as well as the stopping place for all who came to town.

When she looked out the front window she saw great, long piles of hemlock bark for the Frank W. Hunt & Co. tannery, and a long row of "tannery houses" between her house and the river it faced.

"My father used to say he felt like Esau, in the Bible, selling his birthright, when he sold the land for those houses, but he said he could not stand in the way of progress."

When the railroad came through, the Sewalls opened their home to more than forty workers and surveyors. Nancy said they would ring a big bell for meals. Men would come not only from rooms in the house, but also from the stable, hayloft, wagonshed, and a converted henhouse. Nancy's mother, Mary, who was known for her efficiency and patience, remembered the period as "a nightmare." William was unable to find additional help, as he had promised her, so the two of them prepared all the meals. They used a barrel of flour a day.

"The railroad was built the year I was born. This was the only place for people to stay. People always stayed here. The house was always full. My father used to say this house was built on honor, and it was just as solid.

"One time a railroad worker got mad at the paymaster and he was so scared he ran all the way into town and to this house. He did not stop running until he reached the third floor. That's the kind of place this was. The door was always open."

Mary Sewall managed the household, feeding her boarders on "plenty of game" and traveling by boat to Patten for supplies. William farmed and worked in the woods where he bossed some of the log drives on the river. He told his children that the Indians who came down from Canada for the drives were the best bunch of men he had ever worked with.

"I remember when they carried in a woodsman who had been struck by a falling tree. They lay him here on the hearth where it was warm and he died there."

We look silently at the fireplace. A fire has been laid, but it is too warm today to light it. Nancy points to a large black stone on the brick hearth and beckons me to bring it to her. It's a flattened oval about a foot long, polished smooth and shiny, not only by nature, but also by Grandfather Levi Sewall who pounded leather on it when he made shoes. "I imagine a lot of oil has been pounded into this stone," she says, resting it on her knees to demonstrate why it was called a "lapstone."

"There are so many things like this here that are precious to me," she says, "like that grandmother's goose." She points to the door stop—a heavy black, cast-iron pressing iron, one of the two used by Grandmother Rebecca Sewall, who was a seamstress.

Nancy rises from the sofa and leads me through the dining room into a study. Newspaper clippings and pictures are spread out on a studio couch. The walls and shelves display an array of photographs. Half of them are Sewalls. The other half are Roosevelts.

It was fifteen years before Nancy's birth that William Sewall first met Theodore Roosevelt. He was 34 and Roosevelt was 19.

"I never saw him until the inauguration, but Father spoke of him often and was full of admiration. He never called him 'Teddy,' always 'Theodore,' and he said it just so.

"He was a sickly boy when he first stayed at this house. Dr. Arthur Cutler from a boys school in New York brought him the first time. He and a group of New York men had been here to hunt and they told Theodore he should come to Island Falls. He came to the Sewall House three times.

"Father put him through a good many experiences. Long hikes, trips to Katahdin and Munsungan. And when they were camping (on the Mattawamkeag) way down by the dam, Father kept missing him. So he investigated to find out where he was and found him reading his Bible." The place where Theodore read was later named Bible Point and dedicated to his memory.

"We hitched well . . . from the start," wrote Sewall in his *Story of T.R.,* published in 1919. "He was different from anybody that I had ever met; especially, he was fair-minded. He and I agreed in our ideas of fair play and right and wrong.

"The reason that he knew so much about everything, I found, was that wherever he went he got right in with the people . . . Even then he was quick to find the real man in very simple men. He didn't look for a brilliant man when he found me; he valued me for what I was worth."

Nancy recalls how her father and Roosevelt shared a love of poetry and would quote Scott, Whittier, and Longfellow as they tramped the Maine woods and paddled the rivers. Roosevelt's biographer, Charles Putnam, in *The Formative Years 1858-1886*, said that in sixty-nine days in Maine, Roosevelt traversed more than 1,000 miles—330 by wagon, 210 by canoe, and 540 on foot. Most of those miles he traveled with Sewall.

Their friendship deepened, both on camping trips and through a lifelong correspondence. In 1884, not long after Roosevelt's wife and mother died within hours of each other, he hired Sewall and his nephew, Wilmot Dow, to build and manage his Elkhorn Ranch in the Badlands of Dakota.

Nancy brings a small wooden box with a hinged lid from a closet in the study. "I don't want to forget this," she says lifting out a letter with a New York postmark and reading:

School for Boys
40 W. 43rd Street
New York City
My dear Sewall,

Theodore's mother died on Thursday morning at 3 a.m. His wife died the same day at 10 a.m., about twenty four hours after the birth of his daughter.

Of course, the family are utterly demoralized and Theodore is in a dazed, stunned state. He does not know what he does or says. The funeral of both Mrs. Roosevelts took place this morning. A very sad sight. The legislature has adjourned for three days out of respect for Theodore's loss.

Yours Truly,
Arthur H. Cutler

Three weeks later, Sewall received a letter from Roosevelt, inviting him and Dow to join him on his "Western venture."

"Dear Will,—I was glad to hear from you and I know how you feel for me. It was a grim and evil fate, but I have never believed it did any good to flinch or yield for any blow, nor does it lighten the blow to cease from working.

I have thought often of you. I hope my Western venture turns out well. If it does, and I feel sure you will do well for yourself

By coming out with me, I shall take you and Will Dow out next August . . . "

(From Bill Sewall's *Story of T.R.*)

"Such a friendship they had," Nancy reflects. "At the time of the deaths of his mother and his wife, he was so depressed. He said he had nothing to live for. And father said 'you have a daughter and you have everything to live for.' And later, after watching him progress and getting to know him so well, he said 'you could live to be President of the United States.'

"I saw him one other time after the inauguration. He was taking the train to Portland and I was on the same train, coming home from school in Boston. I knew he was on the train and asked the conductor if I might see him.

"'Oh no. The President is not to see anyone.'

"'Well, do you suppose you could just try to tell him that Bill Sewall's daughter, Nancy, is on the train?'

"Shortly, the President's valet came for me and took me to the President's car. All we talked about was my family. He wanted to know how everybody was. The next day it was reported that the President saw only one person during his trip and that was a reporter from a newspaper.

"When I think of him, I think of my father's favorite Bible verse, which became my favorite Bible verse, from Micah:

"'He hath showed me, oh man, what is good, And what doth the Lord require of thee but to do justly, to love mercy and to walk humbly with thy God.'

"As great a man as he was, he always walked humbly with his God."

She finds a large envelope of photographs in the closet and pulls out a large matted photo of Roosevelt on horseback autographed "Theodore Roosevelt, Colonel USV Rough Riders, Spanish-American War." Another photo of a young Roosevelt in an embroidered buck-

The Best of *Echoes* Magazine

skin shirt, fringed fur chaps and alligator boots is labeled "Theodore Roosevelt (President of U.S.A.) about 1882."

I suggest we take the envelope into the living room so we can sit down to examine the rest of its contents. On the way, we stop in the dining room where she has placed two black leather photo albums on a chair. I open one to a page displaying two photos of a teenaged Nancy and a canoe.

"I was at home in a canoe," she says firmly. "Father taught me to respect a canoe from the time I was three years old. He made me my own little paddles and taught me to watch the clouds and the wind and I always have. I was never strong, but I was an outdoor girl."

We add the albums to the envelope of photos and start again for the living room, stopping once more to look at a photo leaning on the sideboard. Three hunters and a dog pose with their overflowing pack baskets of gear. She took the picture.

"For forty-one consecutive years, except one during the war, I went up to the camp hunting. I never killed anything but partridge and a few snakes."

"I had a very happy childhood, and we're still happy," she says. Maurice agrees. "I might not leave footprints in the sands of time, but my life has not been humdrum."

The weather outside resembles the "warm, sunny day" of eighty-five years ago she had just described. The water is running and the sunshine draws our attention out the window.

"I feel sorry for people who cannot see the beauty in a split rail fence," she says. "I feel sorry for people who are in such a hurry to get here and get there that they don't have time to see."

143

A Horse with an Attitude

By Gwen Harmon

My younger sister and I had the pleasant chore of taking Dolly, our pretty little bay pony, to Tom Dow's blacksmith shop in Perham for her annual shoeing. Dad would make the appointment when he had his heavy workhorses in the shop for shoeing or when he was having a piece of machinery repaired. Sometimes he stopped just to banter with the boys who gathered each day to talk and chew tobacco while they watched Tom move ponderously but skillfully about his work.

Doris rode behind me with her short, chubby arms clasped around my waist and her curly towhead peeking around my body so she could see where we were going. We always rode bareback. We grasped Dolly's black mane instead of a saddle horn to keep us from slipping off her back. We pulled out so many handfuls of her coarse long hair that half of her mane would be gone by the end of the summer. Slowly we covered the two miles to the shop. Dolly picked her way carefully along the grassy edge of the road to avoid stepping on sharp stones with her tender feet.

Tom, a short, stocky man with a huge belly bordered by red braces, was never overjoyed to see us coming. Dolly did not like to be shod. When he picked up her front feet to cut the hoof evenly or to place the small iron shoe against her foot for sizing, she would lay her ears back against her head and bite viciously at Tom's large round posterior. When he hesitantly reached for her back foot, she would kick quickly and forcefully. Finally, when he could seize the fetlock firmly and lift her foot off the dirt floor, it was almost impossible for him to hold her short slim leg between his fat, stubby ones and at the same time reach over his broad belly and nail a shoe on the bottom of her constantly moving foot.

He would pick up a flat, iron horseshoe with a pincer-type tool and hold it on the glowing red coals of the forge until the iron was gray-ish white with extreme heat. Then he placed it on the anvil and, with quick blow of a heavy hammer, pounded on each end of the malleable iron shoe until the heel caulks were formed. Then he dunked the shoe into a large container of water. The cold water and hot metal hissed and a cloud of steam rose from the tub. A strong, acrid odor was given off when the still-hot metal came in contact with the hoof. When the shoe was properly shaped and the toe and heel caulks were formed, it was nailed securely to the hoof. Sometimes two or three sizings were necessary before Tom was sure that he had shaped the shoe satisfactorily.

One day when Dolly was giving Tom an especially hard time, he asked Newt Spear, who was sitting nearby enjoying Tom's dilemma and Dolly's antics, to hold the pony's head to one side and stand so her vision of the blacksmith would be blocked. This ploy worked fairly well. Newt chewed on his tobacco and occasionally squirted a stream of the brown juice over his shoulder and onto the dirt floor while Tom continued with his work. Newt shifted the weight of his heavy body with its broad sagging stomach from one leg to the other, spat on the floor and drawled, "She's gut a disposition like Lee Haley, ain't she?"

I was furious to hear such a disparaging remark about our pony and our father. My immediate thought was, "You just wait 'til I tell Dad."

When Dolly had four new shoes on her hooves, I jumped on her and rode over to an old barrel resting on its side. Doris climbed up on the barrel and with an assist from me, managed to swing her short legs over the pony's sides and settle into her place behind me. We kicked the pony's sides with our heels, shook the rope reins to start her into motion and rode slowly out of the shop, up over the hill and back home again.

It was noon when we got back and Dad and the hired man were in from the fields. The workhorses were in their stalls munching on their hay and grain while they switched the horseflies off their sweaty bodies with their long tails. Their feet stamped up and down on the planked floor to keep the flies from biting their tender bellies. We put Dolly in her stall, gave her hay and lots of grain to compensate for Newt's rude remark and ran into the house.

Mom had dinner on the table, and Doris and I slid into our places beside the others who were already eating. Without looking up from his plate, Dad asked, "Did you kids get the pony shod?"

"Yes," I replied and rushed on, "And do you know what that Newt Spear said?" Without waiting for a response, I continued, "He said Dolly had a disposition just like Lee Haley's."

Dad threw his head back and laughed loudly. I stared in amazement. When he stopped laughing, he said, "The next time he says that you tell him Dolly has a belly like Newt Spear's."

Horses
By John Dombek

Joe and I climbed onto the fence that ran along the dirt racetrack where the annual Fourth of July horse pulling contest was to be held. This was a good place to sit. We were close enough to feel the ground vibrate when hooves pounded the dirt, close enough to hear the horses snort with the strain of pulling thousands of pounds of cement piled on the pulling sled, and close enough to hear the farmers order their teams into action.

The first pair of horses was harnessed by thick leather straps that had been polished 'til they gleamed. These were workhorses who earned their day at the fair by plowing, pulling and hauling together all year long. The farmer who owned the team had spent most of the previous day preening the big reds, whose coats, accented by the dark leather straps, glistened in the warm summer sun.

Each team had three pulls at the sled with more weight being added after each pull. The farmer held the reins in one hand with enough leather trailing to serve as a noisemaker or whip in his other hand. He walked his team to the sled with a helper carrying the hitch so it wouldn't drag along the ground. The team was directed carefully to the front of the sled. On signal, the helper dropped the hitch onto the iron ring attached to the sled and leaped out of the way.

"Geeee!! Geeeee!!" The farmer yelled, and Joe and I got goose bumps. "Geeee!!"

The powerful teams would snap up the slack. Chains and harnesses draped on the horses tightened and the magnificent animals leaned into their work. Muscles strained, eyes widened. They seemed to know this was not just another plow they were pulling.

"Geeee!!"

The heavy sled would budge to one side, then the other. Then, as the horses pulled in unison, off it would go, spraying dirt into the air down the track.

"Whoa! Whoa!"

The teams were excited after the pull. When they first approached the sled they'd be quiet and calm. After the pull, adrenaline flowed and only the farmer's voice could calm them and still their desire. They seemed like soldiers after battle, alive with a sense of duty.

On the final pull, the farmers' personalities showed. Each contestant had a chance to win the trophy and the prize money. The win was closer, within reach, and they each showed the desire to own the championship team. This transformed the farmers into competitors who displayed for the crowd the attitude each had for his or her animals.

The gentle farmer with the glistening reds loved his horses. When they put their massive shoulders and haunches into the task and the sled didn't move, the farmer encouraged them with his voice, increasing its intensity, but never to the point of anger. He was like the enthusiastic coach who yelled at his players with admiration for their abilities and recognition for their shortcomings. The tone of his voice inspired his great animals to pull with all their might. It was mutual love. The farmer urged his horses to do their very best because he loved his animals and wanted them to win. And the horses, feeling the gentle hold in their bits, the loose reins and the strong, steady voice of the farmer, strained to their master's bidding because they wanted to please him. Slowly, in perfect harmony, the big reds hauled the sled six long feet.

The farmer with the mammoth Belgians got his team into the finals through sheer meanness. He used the long end of the leather reins as a whip, which he brought down across their straining bodies with angry force. He frightened the huge beasts into frantic action with curses and whipping that raised cruel welts across their haunches.

"Geee! You goddamn lazy bastards! Geee!"

The Belgian team, far outweighing the other two teams in the final pull, could have hauled the sled easily if they had pulled together, but they were so frantic to escape the beating and yelling of the farmer that they pulled opposite each other and failed to get in step. The sled didn't budge. The whistle blew. The farmer cursed.

"Whoa! Whoa! Lazy sons-a-bitches! Whoa!"

The Belgians were panting, snorting and shaking with anxiety. Their eyes were wild, and they continued to jerk and jump as the angry farmer drove them away.

A pair of identical grays also made the final pull. They wore silver tassels near their ears, and silver studs spotted the leather harnesses that draped their huge bodies. They were beautiful, confident horses. They held their heads high and pranced regally in perfect unison to the waiting sled. Their owner was a woman.

"C'mon, girls," she whispered. "C'mon, pay attention."

The hitch dropped into the iron ring, the woman flipped the reins, which slapped the butts of her grays, and they responded. Haunches down and front hooves digging, they heaved into the pull with two great snorts. The front of the sled dug into the dirt. Chunks of mud from the pounding hooves flew into the air and covered the sled. Clouds of dust exploded from beneath their powerful legs.

"C'mon, girls!!!"

The sled moved, slowly, slowly, an inch, two inches, two feet, four, six! That was it. It was all they could do. It was all they needed to do to tie the reds.

"Whoa, girls! Whoa! Good job!"

The final pull was exciting. Best distance out of three pulls got first place. We wanted it to end in a tie, but after three pulls, equal weight, the farmer with the gentle hands and the big-hearted reds out-pulled the grays.

"Nice looking grays."

"We'll get you next year."

"Maybe. Maybe not."

Joe and I jumped off the fence and ran over to the barn where the contestant horses were munching on well-earned lunches. We wanted to stroke their huge noses and feed them some oats out of the palms of our hands. We particularly wanted to stroke the Belgians.

Clearing the Land
By Barry Blackstone

Ray Carter tells this story in his book *An Informal History of Washburn*:

"A preacher came upon a pioneer at work clearing his land on a hot July day. Cutting down trees, digging up roots, clearing stones and stumps was an immense task given the simple tools available to the settler. It was made ever more stressful by the swarms of black flies. The man was a little careless with his language, so the preacher reminded him of Job and the great patience attributed to that prophet. To this unsolicited sermon the man replied, 'Job, he wouldn't have stayed here for five minutes.'"

When I stand on the hallowed homestead of my youth, I recall the tales my grandfather Carroll told of the time he and his brothers, along with his father and grandfather, cleared the land. It is easy in the 1990s to forget how hard it was for the early settlers in Perham. Today, we can stand in open and productive fields, once dense with trees. We know of our ancestors' labors, but can we ever, will we ever, fully understand what it took for them to clear the land with saw and sweat?

The Blackstone Homestead in Perham, Maine, is made up of small fields surrounded by forest. Each of those pieces of ground had to be cleared sometime during the lives of five generations of Blackstones. Huge timbers had to be moved so the first crop of potatoes could be planted. As the years passed, stumps and rocks had to be removed with each new plowing.

I participated in only one clearing during my boyhood on the farm. The land had already been cleared of brush. The trees on that corner of the homestead had been used for firewood. It was a small piece of ground near the Sugar Woods on the Russell Place. It only covered a few acres, but it took me and my cousins and our dads all summer to clear it. I remember Grampa and his brother Read helping. The last field they ever cleared.

The process of turning woodland into farmland was slow. We had to blow stumps and haul away huge rocks, even before the plow could be used. The boulders were transported by rock sled to the stone pile, and the stumps pulled out of the ground were burned. The plows and harrows came next. After each trip by the tractor and harrow we picked the land again and again until a cover crop of oats and clover could be planted.

The tragedy of this story is that land claimed with difficulty is being reclaimed by the forest because of neglect. It hasn't happened on my homestead yet, but I fear the growth that has consumed the farms surrounding mine will soon engulf my clearing.

Cutting Hay
By Cathie Pelletier

The summer I was ten years old Daddy hired me to cut the hay in the fields surrounding our house. He woke me up one bright morning and asked if I wanted the job. Even though I was a notorious tomboy, it was a great honor to be given such a profoundly male task, and so I came hurriedly down to breakfast.

While I ate, Daddy explained what I must do. I would steer the green and yellow John Deere while the big mower clanged along behind. Ordinarily, this was a two-man operation. One man drove the tractor while a second sat on the mower to raise and lower the blade at the end of each row. This would prevent the blade from battering against huge rocks hiding in the grass at the edges of the field. But there were no available men. They were, I imagine, in the woods doing the really rough work. I would be cutting the hay alone, and that suited me just fine.

On the job, I soon fell into a workable routine. At the end of each swath I put the tractor in neutral, climbed down, and ran back to the mower to raise the blade. Then I raced back to the tractor, turned it around, put it in neutral, rushed back to *lower* the blade, climbed back onto the tractor and away! Another row of hay went down. I always kept a sharp eye out for birds, mice, and the occasional scurrying rabbit. In the distance, the St. John River curled blue and cool and inviting. I could hear laughter rising into the air as local kids dove into the water from Cross Rock, that huge megalith across the river. For three days, I mowed hay like that.

On the final field, a large one hidden from the house and road by a gaggle of white pines, Daddy decided to help me. His own workday was over and, with his assistance, the field could be finished sometime after nightfall.

This became one of the most memorable nights of my childhood, the night Daddy and I cut hay by the light of the tractor, by the light of the moon, by the light of the blessed stars glistening overhead. An orange moon had pushed up over the jagged ridge of pines, big and bold and swelling with newness. The tractor strained in the night as it swept back and forth across the black field, leaving behind the sacrificed hay that would feed the workhorses. I was not afraid of the darkness. My father was silhouetted just a few feet away as he steered the tractor. I could see his precious outline, cut sharply by the light of the moon, by the headlights of the tractor, by a daughter's loving eye. I wondered what we would look like from an airplane, little creatures that we were, strutting across our black sea of hay toward some *thing*: the line of trees, the moon, the finished job, the day I would grow up and leave it all behind.

I have carried this memory around the world, and I have conjured it up during the most severe bouts with homesickness. "Oh, Daddy," I have wondered, thousands of miles from the scene. "Can you still see the moon, as I can? Do you hear the tractor's sweet cough, and the quick teeth of the blade eating up the hay? Those were *years* falling, Father, those blades of grass we passed through so quickly there is now no trace that we were ever there."

The White Pine

By Francis X. Bolton

I am standing in my kitchen in Brooklyn, New York, jacket on, keys in hand when the phone rings.

"Mr. Bolton."

"Yes."

"You'll sleep better tonight."

I think telephone solicitation. "Who is this, please?"

"Steve Gray—from Danforth."

It takes but a second for it to click. "The tree is down," I say.

"Took her down this morning. There was no wind so I called Micah Bartlett to see if he was free. We hauled her up on the bank."

"That's great."

The tree Steve is talking about is 569 miles northeast, in Orient, Maine, smack in front of my camp, five feet from the house, five feet from the lake. The tree has been on my mind for years. *Echoes* published a poem of mine in Issue 92 (2011) where I express a hope the tree is diseased; that would mean I could fell the tree. My one regret in the poem is that the fledgling eagle I'd seen land on its lower branches might no longer visit us.

"Seven trips to the dump," Steve says. "The trunk is in three pieces; twenty-one feet, seventeen feet and eleven feet long. They're lying right alongside the house."

"Terrific. I'll call the fellow from the mill."

The phone call over, relief washes over me. For several years, I'd had the occasional vision of a summer when my wife and I would be crushed by a huge pine bough while we slept.

A number of years prior, when I first discussed the tree with Mike Noble, the code enforcement officer, he told me the tree was still healthy. When I pointed to the stump of another very tall white pine at the rear of the property, explaining what had happened to that tree, he was unmoved.

"It was dead and the power company took it down for me," I told him. You don't need permission to take down a dead tree, even if it is within one hundred feet of the shoreline.

I then pointed to the stump of a spruce in the nook of our house. "That was healthy," I told him, "but it leaned into the house over the winter. See the new shingles?" The spruce was two feet from one wall and three feet from the other. "See that semicircle of broken roots?" I had gotten permission to take that down because it was dangerous.

"Look at all these trees." I gesture to the thirty or more trees on our one-hundred-feet by one-hundred-and-ten-feet property.

Mike said that, with its abundance of trees, this is ideally what an older camp should be like. "There isn't any brown on that pine's needles," Mike said. "You can't take the tree down."

He was pleasant enough, but unrelenting.

I was seeking permission to cut it down because it had been dropping branches on our roof over the preceding years. Just like the pine at the back of our property had, the pine the power company took down when, despite hopeful pruning, it died.

Well, the pine in front of our house wasn't so obliging. It continued dropping branches each winter. One year there were four of them on the roof, yet the tree continued to live. Each year they fell from a greater and greater height.

Each year after that conversation with Mike, I'd climb onto the roof looking for the tiny holes fallen branches might have poked in it. The last summer before the tree came down, I couldn't locate them all. One morning after a torrent the previous evening that filled two wastebaskets full of water, and after mopping, mopping, mopping the floor, I went out to measure the circumference of the pine tree. Alone. My wife was with friends on the coast. I was assembling data to plead my case to fell the tree: photos of fallen branches, arranged in year order; photos of the holes in the roof that I had succeeded in finding; photos showing that there were no branches overhanging the house for the first forty feet up, they'd all snapped off; photos of a widow-maker fifty feet up that was a devil to get down; photos of the hill you walked up, and then down, when you walked over the trees' roots. The circumference of the tree was the last bit of data.

Have you ever tried to measure the circumference of a really large tree alone? Just as I was thinking I'd have to wait until my wife returned, I heard a voice: "Need a hand there?" Steve Gray from Danforth. He was leveling my neighbor's camp.

"Thinking of taking this tree down?" he asked when we finished measuring.

I tell him my story.

"I can take it down." He said he could climb it and cut it down in sections, which is what I'd prefer. If the tree kicked as it toppled, it could knock in the front wall of the house.

"And tell Mike that Steve from Danforth says the tree isn't stable."

So I called Mike and left a message on his cellphone. Two weeks later, with no return call, I left a second message. "We're heading south soon."

Before we left, I told Alicia Silkey (Lisi) at the Orient Town Office about the tree. She called Mike. Her message was "I have a resident here, Mr. Bolton, who has a tree in front of his house." As a footnote, she adds, "Someone down in Danforth who works with trees told him it's not stable." As I left the office, Lisi said she would see Mike in mid-September at a selectmen's meeting. I filed that information away.

Weeks later, still no word. I called Lisi on September 17. "It's fine," she says. "I asked Mike, 'What about Mr. Bolton's tree?' and he said, 'He can take it down.'" I moved into the tree-cutting phase.

I reminded Steve that I want to save the cedar trees that grow on the bank under the pine's branches (that is how large this pine tree is). He will wait for the lake to freeze hard enough to drop it on the ice. We agreed on a price.

Then I called Steve Hopkins in Hodgdon. Our friend Dick Rhoda told me Steve H. owns a small lumber mill that specializes in exotic woods. "That pine is straight. Maybe he would be interested." Steve H. said he would take the tree if it was sound. We agreed on a price per thousand board feet.

In mid-January, I called Steve G. to ask when he would cut down the tree. "The lake isn't hard enough yet."

I called him again in mid-February. "I drove by the other day and looked at the tree."

I waited.

"It's a really big tree."

"I know."

I skipped a beat before asking, "Do you want to take it down?"

"No, I'm thinking maybe I should just drop it."

And I'm thinking maybe I should have called the guys in Vanceboro who would have climbed the tree. But a deal is a deal.

"If there is no wind, I think it would come right down."

Once the tree was down, I called Steve H. at the sawmill.

"Maybe you want to look at it," I suggested. He doesn't pick up trees; I need to get it delivered to him and I don't want it rejected at the mill. He drove down a few days later and reported he would take the whole thing. The lengths are great. The twenty-one-foot and eleven-foot lengths can be cut into ten-foot boards and the seventeen-foot length into eight-foot boards.

I called Joe Ledger in Amity. He took away the pine tree the power company had cut down. It takes me a few days to catch him at home but when I do, he says, "I'd like the work but there is a problem."

I'm thinking maybe he sold his truck but no, the road is posted. "I drove past there the other day," Joe tells me.

The only thing I know about posting is "POSTED. No Trespassing" or "No Hunting." I never heard of a posted road. I discover roads are posted in the winter for a maximum weight limit and the road going past my camp is posted at a maximum of 26,500 pounds.

"So once you load the tree on, you'd be too heavy?"

"Without a load, my truck weights 32,600 pounds."

So I called Steve H. in Hodgdon and explained the situation. I don't tell Steve that Joe had told me the road to his mill is also posted. "It might be a while before I can get the tree to you."

"Well, that's a problem."

I believe him because, well, what do I know? But what possibly could be wrong with waiting a few days or weeks?

"Blue mold."

"Blue mold?"

"Yes. Pine trees get blue mold." If I remember correctly, it's not visible when the tree is delivered to the mill; it appears when the weather gets fairly hot. But if the wood is milled early enough, it doesn't occur.

"To avoid blue mold, I don't take pine trees in a month that doesn't have an 'R' in it." I think March, April.

"Do you ever make an exception?"

"Call me when the road isn't posted and we'll talk about it."

I think of what a fine tree it is, straight and broad. I think of it as enormous. And May is only eight days away.

So I called Alicia in the town office. "Do you know when the posting on the road will be lifted?" She doesn't but will keep track of it. About a week later, she calls to say one of the locals is logging down that road so the posting must have been lifted.

I call Steve H. at the mill and he says he would take the tree even though it is May 2.

I call Joe in Amity and leave him a message that the road is no longer posted. And on May 4, I get a call from the mill saying they have the tree.

That summer, when I go to the mill to meet Steve H. and collect three long, thick boards he has set aside for me, boards I will have made into a table, one with a history associated with the camp, I see some pine boards delicately streaked with blue mold. I wish my boards had some.

Amish Neighbors
By Kathryn Olmstead

When Carla Hayes of Fort Fairfield learned an Amish family had bought the farm down the road, she could hardly wait for them to move in.

"When the news was out that the Amish were coming to our community, just three houses from where I live, I had an intense excitement and interest to meet these people and really did not understand why. Now, four years later, my understanding is very clear," she said, in 2011.

"Noah and Lovina (Yoder) and their eleven children have become wonderful friends and we are blessed to have them as neighbors. The impact this family has had on my husband, David, and me has been deep, more than an ordinary relationship."

In 2007, Amish families began moving into the communities of Fort Fairfield and Easton from New York, Ohio, Iowa, Kentucky, and Missouri. Representing one of the most conservative Amish orders, they live without electricity and telephones and use only horse-powered vehicles and farm equipment. They speak a dialect of German (also called Pennsylvania Dutch) to each other and English to their neighbors, whom they call "the English." Facing the lens of a camera offends not only their modesty and privacy, but also their religious beliefs.

Parents in this community have as many as fourteen children, whom they educate in a one-room school through grade eight, when young people begin their chosen work. Each family pursues a particular trade for income—carpentry, metalwork, harness making, baking—as well as farming for sustenance.

Drawn to Aroostook County by its remoteness and the availability of affordable farmland, the Amish cultivate the small fields, unsuitable for large farm equipment, that have lain fallow in the wake of corporate consolidation of agriculture.

"They are increasing the value of the land tremendously," said Steve Ulman, who owns the Rocking S Ranch and riding stables in Fort Fairfield. "We have so much land in Aroostook County, yet we have fewer people. Now we have people coming in who value the land. As agriculture moves away from labor-intensiveness, they are cultivating small farms still capable of producing wonderful crops. They are like a transfusion."

Former Fort Fairfield town manager Dan Foster agreed.

"They know how to do community, among themselves and the English—how to resolve issues and work together for the common good. There are a lot of lessons to be learned," he said, describing their collaborative decision-making and easy, gentle way of doing business. "People are seeing that, and it can't help but rub off and make you feel better about your community."

Sustainable economic development is about more than jobs and infrastructure, Foster said. It's creating a place of quality where people want to be and want to participate in the community. The Amish contribute to that quality of life.

"They live their values and demonstrate how to utilize a shared resource. They bring out the best in people. They bring out people's desire to help. I love having them here. They are wonderful people."

Carla and David Hayes feel the warmth of their Amish neighbors daily. "Our ways of living are years apart," Carla said, "however their examples of family, neighbors and community are very 'today,' or, should I say, the way it should be in our state now. Never would there be a need for a welfare system or a need to draw on other government resources if we learned from their ways, starting with family."

As she anticipated the arrival of the Amish, Carla worried about how to communicate, wondering if they would be shy and unwilling to make eye contact.

"Welcome!" she shouted from her front yard the first time she saw a horse-drawn wagon approach. The driver pulled the horses to a halt. A man climbed down and walked around the wagon hand outstretched.

"I'm Harvey Miller," he said, looking her straight in the eye with a smile.

So much for that myth, she thought.

Harvey and his brother-in-law, Noah Yoder, were the first to arrive with their families from Heuvelton, New York, in August 2007. Their Amish brethren elsewhere doubted they could endure the cold and remote northern Maine winter and they wanted to test their resiliency. It was the year of the big snow.

"It was the best winter of my life," Noah recalled almost four years later on the day Carla took me to visit the Yoder farm. The cold was no worse than in northern New York, and Aroostook was the perfect setting for raising their children—a farm-based lifestyle conducive to teaching responsibility at an early age.

"We couldn't have hoped for a better community," Noah said, describing the warm welcomes that greeted them when they arrived. "For a whole month, not a day went by when people didn't stop by with food or offers of help. We had to improve our way of living. People up here were better at it than we were.

"Sandy Gagnon made our move so much easier," he said of the Key Real Estate agent he dealt with. "I can't say enough good things about her." He laughed when he recalled her response to his first letter of inquiry. She asked him to send her his cellphone number and email address.

As Carla, Noah and I talk in the doorway of his carpentry shop, eleven-year-old Joni steers a team of workhorses out of the dooryard and onto the road toward the field where he will "tet" the hay, or rake it into rows for drying. With a weekend of warm days forecasted, haying is a priority.

The Yoders farm about one-hundred acres and maintain a store selling baked goods, produce and souvenirs. They provide milk destined for commercial distribution, and their one concession to electricity is the line providing power to the cooler for the milk. They use stationary gas engines for belt-driven power tools, but not for transportation. They travel on the ground, but not in the air.

A car drives into the Yoder dooryard and a couple hops out saying they found something they think Noah might like. He need not feel obligated to buy it, but they thought of him when they saw it at a yard sale. They open the trunk and lift out a scythe with two extra blades. Noah accepts the traditional tool gratefully in a transaction symbolic of the relationship between the Amish and their Aroostook County neighbors.

Paul Cyr of Presque Isle is among the county residents who have developed strong ties with members of the Amish community. He has helped them with small earth construction projects, and he frequently stops by with the morning weather forecasts, information important for farming but unavailable to those without radio or television. Paul's first contact with the Amish families grew from his talent as a photographer.

"Noah wanted me to take pictures of the high snowbanks (during that first winter in Aroostook) to send back to their friends in New York," he said. That assignment laid the groundwork for a trust that has enabled him to take numerous pictures in the community.

"We work with each other. They know I won't mess with them," he said, meaning he will not photograph their faces.

But Noah said the day Paul appeared in the sky hanging from a powered parachute it was hard not to look at him, especially for the children. Paul has created hundreds of images of the Amish, and even produced an Amish calendar that outsold scenic calendars twenty to one until the Bishop frowned on it and production was discontinued.

"Part of the mystique is I don't show their faces," Paul said, explaining that his images of the Amish are the most popular in his archive. "It's a unique little world of its own."

It is a world that is growing within Aroostook County. In addition to Fort Fairfield and Easton, Amish families have made homes in Smyrna, Oakfield, Bridgewater, and Stacyville. Noah helps spread the word about Aroostook County settlements as a correspondent for *Botschaft*, the nationally distributed Amish weekly newspaper. His articles, mailed in as hand-written submissions, report upcoming events, such as barn-raisings and weddings that may attract visitors from other states as well as other parts of Maine.

Amish craft is becoming part of northern Maine culture as products of their workshops and kitchens appear in more and more places in Aroostook County. Furniture, storage sheds, harnesses, metalwork, straw hats, as well as baked goods are becoming more familiar as Amish businesses prosper.

Mattie Yoder, Noah's niece, operates a store on the busy corner of Routes 1A and 10 in Easton, representing the next generation of Amish business owners in Aroostook. The store offers a variety of locally produced goods.

"The Amish have been successful at what we are unable to do—keep our young people in Aroostook," observed Steve Ulman. "That speaks volumes."

Noah explained that children are given responsibility at an early age, beginning with tasks such as caring for an animal. "The earlier you learn to take responsibility the better you are," he said. "There is no manual for raising children. What is often missing is real love for children."

Carla recalled the day two of Noah's children appeared at the door shortly after their father had passed by and noticed David in the yard stacking wood.

"We have been sent to ask if we can help," they said with smiles. This gesture is an example of the neighborliness that has impressed the Hayes family. "There is an element of sharing, helping and caring that is taught as the foundation for adulthood," Carla observed. "There is joy in being able to help. They are the greatest example of what community should be—to help and care for one another."

The Moose in my Backyard
By Mary Warren

I had lived in Aroostook County only a few weeks when I had to fly to Boston on business. On my first return flight back to Presque Isle, the plane landed with a tremendous *kerfumph*, followed by several gigantic bumps as we hopped from the runway back up into the air at least seven times, finally settling into a steady *s-c-r-e-e-e-c-h* as the pilot leaned heavily on the brakes and we smoked down the runway . . . right past the terminal.

We slowed enough to make a 180-degree turn and headed back to the terminal. It is a small airport with rather large runways, which may explain why the pilot was so liberal with his landing speed. Actually, the runways are long for the type of aircraft I had been riding in because Presque Isle's airport is located on a former Air Force Base. It is a grand runway for a small airport. The terminal is tiny but very nice with a neat little aircraft museum.

I made my way to the baggage claim area. In most cities, this is a stressful experience as one waits to see if the luggage is there at all, and then of course, if it is in one piece. Not so at the airport in Presque Isle, Maine.

Before leaving, I had parked my car out front and run into the terminal to ask about long-term parking. Like, where was it?

"Oh, it's right over there," I was told.

"Excuse me, sir," I pressed the happy-faced nineteen-year-old behind the counter (lately everyone looks nineteen to me). "But exactly where would that be?"

"Oh, you can park anywhere," he replied.

"Well, isn't there some sort of overnight charge for parking?" I asked.

"Oh, yes, madam," he said.

"And how much would that be?"

"Two dollars a night, but you don't have to pay it now. You can just pick up an envelope and send it in anytime. It's the honor system."

Once again, I was reminded of why I moved here. This is not "quaint"—this is real. I once lived in New York City and worked at the World Trade Center, on the 107th floor, way before 9/11, and I can tell you that there is no honor system about money in the city. A lot of wonderful people, yes, but a money honor system? Never.

So, after deplaning, I dashed out to my car and pulled it up to the front entrance of the terminal and left it running, yes, left it running and unlocked, while I ran back in for my baggage.

I smiled inwardly at the "congestion" at the one baggage belt—maybe twenty people standing around waiting for luggage. I retrieved mine, got my envelope for the honor-system-overnight-parking, and returned to my still-running car; yes, still running and still there, outside the terminal. I tossed my suitcase into the back seat, climbed into the toasty comfort of my auto, and started the sixty-four-mile drive to my home in Fort Kent.

Along the way, I stopped in Caribou for some shopping. Boston didn't offer the real north-country shoes I wanted. Comfortable, warm and practical, that is the hallmark of this land, no matter what you are purchasing. I had been told about a place in Caribou called Sleeper's where these types of things can be had at a reasonable price. Thinking it was something like L.L. Bean, I looked it up.

It is not exactly like L.L. Bean; actually it is what Bean's used to be like, back when I was a kid. Nothing upscale here, it is frugal, practical and has a grocery store attached. Lobsters were on sale. They had a sign telling where the current batch of lobsters came from, and that week they were from Vinalhaven.

Since I had to spend three hours at the Boston airport before departure due to security, I had picked up Linda Greenlaw's book, *The Lobster Chronicles*. Of course, I read and relished every page thinking how parallel our recent lives seemed. She moved back to her birthplace in Maine, Isle au Haut, to fish lobster and I've moved back to Maine via Fort Kent, to what? View moose? Perhaps I should write the Moose Chronicles, I thought during the bumpy flight back.

Regardless, when I saw the terrific price for lobsters at Sleeper's, I decided to buy one—a big guy—almost three pounds! Even though I was alone, what the heck, why not celebrate my return to the north country? Yum, I thought, a giant Maine lobster for dinner! I picked up Evie (my trusty Jack Russell terrier) at the dog sitter, no kennel for my little girl, and together we climbed up to the third hill on South Perley Brook Road. It had been my first time away.

How happy I was to be home. I felt safe. After only a few days in Boston, I really looked forward to being cocooned in the St. John Valley.

I unpacked and began boiling water for my lobster dinner. I was standing at the sink when I glanced up and out the window to see a huge dark figure trotting steadily at a diagonal across the meadow and down the hill directly behind the house. I turned off the water, grabbed the loose lobster, now wandering around the countertop, and ran to the French doors in the dining area leading to the rear deck. I had opened both doors to release the steam from the boiling pots. Dressed in an Old Town Canoe apron and holding a lobster in one hand and a wooden spoon in the other, I tramped out onto the deck to see a moose, a bull moose.

He was beautiful, with a wide and full rack. I was so excited, I backed through the French doors and into the house tripping over the half-step and dropping the lobster onto the floor. In trying to be quiet, I had made such a commotion that the moose stopped in his tracks and came directly towards the deck! He lowered his neck and cocked his head as if to get a better look at the crazy lady with a tremendous spider at her feet, waving a giant spoon in the air!

I felt completely at odds and out of sorts next to this magnificent creature. That did not keep me from acting. With the lobster crawling up my foot and the moose barely ten feet from the deck, I called my dog!

Now Evie is all of twenty pounds, but she is a Jack Russell terrier, the kind of dog who will not give up . . . under any circumstances. Tired from her weekend away, she had been sound asleep under the covers in my bed. But at the sound of my shrill command, she came dashing out of the bedroom, across the foyer, through the living room and around the corner to the dining room . . . to save me.

She didn't see the moose, but she certainly saw the lobster sashaying across the floor. She raced over to it and tried to pick it up. Seeing what she was going for, I grabbed for it myself. She beat me to it and when she tried to pick the huge, hard-shelled thing up in her mouth, she bit off one of the rubber bands holding one of the claws shut.

I snatched the hapless thing from her, swirled around and lunged for the doors. Evie had now spied the moose and was headed straight toward the open door. The moose had moved closer and was standing at the step to the deck just staring at me.

Oh my! Would he try to come into the house? I reached out with my free hand as quickly as I could in order to close the doors. With my other hand, I caught Evie just as she tried to dart past me. Unfortunately, that meant I had to drop the lobster again, since I only have two hands.

Now that he had a free pincer claw, it took a split second for him to grab the front of my Old Town Canoe apron and the sweatshirt beneath, and just hang there, legs hammering away, up and down, up and down. I let out a scream which evidently spooked the moose, because with a wave of his head he turned and bucked, that's right, bucked, rather playfully, I thought, and cantered away.

Evie barked hysterically and clamored at the doors. The irate lobster clamped to my apron would not let go. I didn't care.

With lobster dangling from my breast, I stood at those French doors for a rather long time smiling and watching. After all, you can get lobster any old time, but a moose in your backyard, now that's really something.

Rubbing Elbows
By Dorothy Boone Kidney

Stan's is not dolled up to resemble an old store. It is an old store. As soon as you park in front of the place on the east shore of Madawaska Lake, you notice the moss on the roof and the tilt of the building, tired from sitting for so many generations. Men linger on the weathered bench out front, talking about the weather or the fishing, or just waiting for the mailman to stuff the mail into the boxes beside the front door for residents around Madawaska Lake—T16, R4, Maine.

When you walk into Stan's, you are walking back in time about one-hundred years. The interior is not chintzy, not cute, but shadowy, restful and dim, with shelves of old household cleaners, canned goods, suspenders, fly dope, mixing spoons, hunting caps, penny candy, kerosene lamps, greeting cards. You name it. Stan Thomas, bearded and jovial, says, "If we don't have it, you don't need it."

Against the back wall, an ancient piano with an array of plants, faded pictures and paper flowers on the top occasionally inspires someone to play a lively song or a hymn, or even to accompany a solo. Customers often join in.

Three old booths, the seats of which tip a little bit, overlook the lake. Two tables, one long and one round, are covered with plastic cloths. Stan and his sister, Emilie, cook breakfasts and lunches in a small kitchen. Eggs, bacon and ham are cooked the way you like them, and served with toasted homemade bread and home-style jelly. Everyone knows everyone and newcomers become acquainted quickly with the lake folk and people from Stockholm, New Sweden, Westmanland, and other towns nearby. People have their own reasons for coming to Stan's.

Donna Cochran and her husband, George, have a cabin on the north shore of Madawaska Lake. She says she likes the ease of visiting.

"At Stan's you can socialize with friends and feel free to leave when you want to. In someone's home or cottage, you sometimes feel you must stay a bit longer out of politeness. At Stan's you can leave easily whenever you want to, without explanation or apology."

Pat and Saul Levasseur have returned to Madawaska Lake from their home in Westfield, Massachusetts, for 12 years, and Pat has tried to figure out why Stan's fascinates her.

"I've sat on that old picnic table across the road and looked over at this ancient, sagging building and puzzled about it. I guess it's because there are always people here when you come in, a different crowd of people at different times of day.

"There are early breakfast people, then morning mail people, then cribbage people gathered around the long table—a cross-section of people. An old man walks in, sits down at a booth for coffee, and is surrounded with familiar faces. Yet, Saul and I stopped in one day in the afternoon and didn't know a single person here at that time of day. Yes, I guess it's the crowds of people at different times of day."

The mixing of people, the old-fashioned homeyness, and memories associated with Stan's appeal to Bud Anderson. He gestures to the lake outside the window.

"I caught my first fish—a fourteen-inch salmon—out there when I was six years old, on a fishline off my dad's reel with a hook and sinker. I can still feel the alder pole against the pit of my stomach. I've been coming to this region for over sixty years," he continued. "There's a whole lifetime in this place. When I first started coming to the area with my parents, we rode in an open touring car. Going through Jemtland swamp, Mother used to say, 'Keep your arms inside the car so you won't get hurt,' because the bushes grew so close to the edges of the narrow road."

Looking at the lake from Stan's window evoked memories of Anderson's teenaged years when he rented a boat and rowed his girlfriend across the lake. He rowed his wife, Joanie, too, but "she wouldn't let me take her so far out that she couldn't see the bottom." He and Joanie were married in 1945 and in 1952 they built their own cottage on the lake, where they have lived ever since. "I did the sawing and fitting and Joanie did the hammering."

"The interest here for me," said Phil Harmon, another year-round resident, "is the big-family-around-the-table feeling. A lot of us have known one another for years. It's the old country store with the cracker barrel and wood-burning-stove atmosphere." He pointed to the gas light on a post in the dining area. "Instead of the wood-burning stove, though, we have this gas light. "It's the camaraderie I like," Harmon added. "It's a place to gather, to catch up on all the current news. I have a name for it. I call it the Social and Cultural Center of Madawaska Lake.

Eldon and Laura Giles of Mapleton were married in the rain at Madawaska Lake on Roland St. Peters' party boat. "The boat had a canopy," he recalled, "but the wind blew the rain in. The minister asked, 'What do we do?' and I said, 'Get wet.' We got drenched, but it was a good wedding."

Giles summarized the attraction of Stan's in two words: "Fellowship and friendship. Oh, yes, and the ten-cent coffee. It's important to people to get together."

Lena Wardwell and Selena Ouellette reflected the harmonious mix of ages at Stan's. Both seven years old, they skipped in and sat in the booth next to mine, Lena's red hair bouncing and Selena's brown eyes dancing.

"Do you like coming here?" I asked.

"Oh yes!" Lena exclaimed. "It's fun. They have lots of candy and bubble gum and ice cream with chocolate chips!"

Selena praised the cheeseburgers. "And I like to come here swimming," she added, pointing to the beach outside the window. Lena's dad showed up with the food. "Which one of you wants to pray?" he asked. They hesitated, so he thanked the Lord for the cheeseburgers and chips.

Teenagers also gather at Stan's. Buffy Plourde, who lives at Madawaska Lake year round, said she rides her bike two miles to get to the store and sometimes brings a friend.

"They're really nice people and they have great cheeseburgers."

Between customers, Stan joined me in my booth by the window and explained that he bought the store in 1964. "Sodergren built it a little before the turn of the century. Rumberg owned it after that, then Lawson, then Chester Buzzell, now me. "Being up here kind of grows on you," he said. "I don't know whether I could ever return to the farm. Maybe the first couple of nights, looking out the window back in 1964 and waiting for something to happen was sort of doubtful and hard, but it wasn't long before things began to happen.

"When I first came up here, I made up my mind if I couldn't help people, I'd go back to Caribou. I was told twenty-eight years ago if I didn't put in beer, I wouldn't last a month. It just proves, you don't have to have beer."

Stan described how he tries to anticipate the needs of his customers. "It's eighteen miles to Caribou. If they can pick it up here, fine. We decided we wouldn't sell anything we didn't want ourselves, and we wouldn't overprice things."

"Like your ten-cent coffee?"

"Like our ten-cent coffee. And there's something I learned years ago about serving food—it doesn't cost any more to go fresh. I try to buy native as much as I can."

Stan acknowledged that he provides more than food and merchandise, that there is something else that attracts folks.

"Peace of mind, for one thing," he observed. "There's something about sitting here beside the windows and watching the water that's soothing. And friendship is another. In the lower part of the state, people often don't know who their neighbors are. It's not like that around here. People know and help one another. And people from all walks of life rub elbows in this place. There should be a few more places like it."

"Do you feel that something is lacking in the world out there that causes people to gather here?" I asked.

"Yes, I do," he said. "Most places are geared today around the almighty dollar. They don't have time for small talk any more out in the world. Here people are known by name. Oh, every once in a while a strange face appears, but if they stay around, they don't remain strangers long. They come because they want to talk, but at the same time they don't want to talk. But when they relax and do talk, they find interest, friendship and sometimes advice."

In the wintertime, Stan's attracts snowmobilers and cross-country skiers from the snowmobile trail under the nearby power line and a ski trail called the Island Trail because it is surrounded on three sides by water and by the road on the other side. And when election time rolls around, the end booth is curtained off for voting. "We get about 35 or 36 percent turnout," Stan said.

Sometimes, when local people return, having been away all winter, they stop at Stan's before going home.

"Maybe it's because we are family-oriented here," he said. "My sister Emilie, her husband, Henry, my brother Robert, and my mother and father, Enid and Al Thomas, all help out in the store and we try to follow the Golden Rule."

One of the major reasons my husband, Milford, and I bought an old cabin on Madawaska Lake was that it was just around the corner from Stan's. The moment the owner showed us the cabin (one of the oldest on the lake), with the beaver pelt beside the stone fireplace, the two kerosene lamps on the shelf, and the bear hide thrown carelessly over the railing of the loft, I knew immediately I wanted that kind of world. It was an extension of the world symbolized by Stan's.

The small, family-run grocery store on Main Street has just about disappeared from every town. Little stores where you are known by name have given way to big, impersonal shopping malls. The local hotel, where townfolk socialized in the lobby and the dining room, has been torn down or converted to offices or apartments in many towns.

Still, people are social by nature and need a gathering place for friendly conversation, especially in our modern society. Stan's seems to fulfill this need. A woman from Fort Fairfield told me, "I come here when I get depressed." She had found an antidote for loneliness, and it cost a lot less than a psychiatrist.

Down Home Dinners
By Kathryn Olmstead

Avis Dudley of Castle Hill, Maine, was eighty-one in 1977 when she was featured in *Yankee Magazine* as "the woman who has cooked and served over 115,000 meals in her own home." She called her farmhouse on the Dudley Road an "eating place," telling *Yankee* writer Allen R. Melvyn, "I never consider we're anything like a restaurant because in a restaurant they go in in the morning and make up a main dish and people come and go. We're an eating place."

Thirty-seven years later, her patrons still remember the meals and the atmosphere that made her eating place famous. In October 2014, I wrote a column for the *Bangor Daily News* about her cookbook, *Ma Dudley's Secrets of the Dudley Homestead*, now a collector's item. Reader after reader wrote to tell me they still have and use her cookbook and still hold fond memories of dining in her farmhouse.

"You have made my day," wrote Kathleen Rusley from Augusta, Maine. "Avis is my grandmother. I have the cookbook—given to me as a wedding present. I was able to find several more on eBay to give to my children."

Fort Fairfield native Sharon Barker said her copy of the cookbook was autographed by Avis Dudley on December 15, 1977. "It's in pretty rough shape because it's been well-used, but it is still intact," she said, calling Ma Dudley's "a unique dining experience."

Another reader remembered visits to Ma Dudley's between 1977 and 1980 when her husband was stationed at the former Loring Air Force Base. "The sticky buns and lobster were my favorite," wrote Christy Seckman. "It was nice to sit there all evening long enjoying the fun, food and friends."

Mrs. Dudley served about twenty to thirty people at a time in the dining and living rooms of her husband's ancestral farmhouse, about ten miles from Presque Isle. Guests ordered their meals when they made their reservations, selecting from a menu that included chicken, salmon, ham, pork chops, roast beef, turkey, Cornish game hen, Alaskan king crab legs, lobster, shrimp and duck. She offered four to six entrees at a time. Each meal began with a salad, which she "built" instead of tossing, and a plate of hot caramel rolls, for which she was famous.

She served "family style"—large platters of meat and serving dishes of locally grown vegetables—with her granddaughter and high school students waiting tables. Her kitchen contained four stoves, each with two ovens. Refrigerators, freezers and a walk-in cooler were located elsewhere in the house.

The *Bangor Daily News* column reminded Castle Hill resident Dana Allison of the first time she and her family ate at Ma Dudley's. In her words:

"The first time we had dinner there we did not have a babysitter. Thus, the reason for taking our three-year-old twin boys, Orpheus and Ewen, and our newborn girl, Piper, along with us. Piper was old enough for solid food, and as the kitchen crew prepared our dinner, I was feeding Piper from her jar of prepared baby food. Horace and I were talking about this and that. Suddenly we realized that the boys had disappeared!

"I gave Horace the spoon and told him to continue feeding Piper while I went looking for the boys. I found them! In the kitchen! Ma Dudley was entertaining them as she opened the oven to let them peer into it. I was embarrassed and apologized as I gathered up the boys.

"She said, 'Oh, I enjoy these boys. They are so good.' She went on, "When my husband and I had small children we took them with us, too. If we went anywhere where people presumed that they would act up, be obstreperous, my children didn't disappoint 'em!'"

Ma Dudley's Homestead was popular with military personnel from the former Loring Air Force Base in Limestone and with local and visiting businesspeople who returned again and again.

"What makes me happiest is when people from the (military) service say they have eaten around the world and this is the best food they have ever had," Mrs. Dudley told me for an article that appeared in the *Bangor Daily News* May 18, 1977, when I was a news correspondent.

That feature previewed the cookbook that would become a prized possession of those who purchased it in 1977. Gene and Margaret Wright of Presque Isle edited and printed the book from pages of handwritten recipes Mrs. Dudley delivered to Wright Printing.

"Avis drove up in her light blue Mercury Cougar, a sporty car for a woman her age," Gene recalled. "She brought in a full-sized, hard-sided blue Samsonite suitcase filled with her recipes handwritten on yellow legal pads."

Margaret helped her organize them into sections: breakfast, salads, breads, soups and chowders, vegetables, meats and fish, main dish and desserts. Then they selected anecdotes to include with the recipes.

"I would do it again," Margaret said, adding that the anecdotes were a highlight for her.

Gene and Margaret will never forget the day Mrs. Dudley went on the air to promote the cookbook in an interview with local radio show host Dewey DeWitt. She told listeners that after the show she was heading over to Wright Printing where she would be happy to sign copies of the cookbook.

That was news to the Wrights. The pages for the first two thousand copies of the book had been printed, but they had not yet been collated or spiral bound.

"We had about six copies done," Gene recalled. Not to worry. As the print shop filled with eager customers, Mrs. Dudley kept them entertained in conversation while Gene and Margaret scrambled to assemble the books.

She liked to recall how she got started in November 1963, when the Mapleton Lions Club asked if they could meet at her home twice a month. "They enjoyed themselves and I enjoyed having them," she wrote in an introduction to the cookbook.

The next May she had requests from 18 people for dinner on Mother's Day. That summer, she served various women's groups and other small groups on occasion. "In a year or two I was very well started in a pleasant small venture of my own," she wrote. "It's always a pleasure to see the happy faces of my guests as they leave my home."

One such guest remembered a visit to Ma Dudley's as "one of the most memorable meals of my life," expressing her delight in acquiring a copy of the cookbook in a review on Amazon. "Not only do you get her recipe collection, but the photos, snippets on daily life and folk wisdom are a bonus of insight on another era. You had to be there to truly appreciate the traditional food favorites and hospitality afforded guests, but this cookbook is the best keepsake that I could ever have."

Clean-up
By Davis Chung

My early years were submerged in a powerful symbol of the Cold War, the Strategic Air Command. SAC counted my father as one of its warriors. It took him to Vietnam twice and, at regular intervals, placed him on alert. SAC was the ready force of nuclear-armed B-52s who, without hesitation, would answer the sounds of the siren and fly off to participate in the end of our civilization.

It was something about which you rarely talked or even allowed yourself to dwell upon—how your father's job could signal the end of the world. A SAC crew member once jokingly told me, "We are paid to practice and if we ever really went off and did our job, we've seen our last paycheck anyway."

Loring Air Force Base was one of the nuclear spears that helped keep the larger peace in the years following World War II. The closest continental base to Moscow, it was duly accorded tight security with multiple fences, guards, guns and dogs.

I recall taking a college friend around Loring back when The Bomb still ruled. While stopped at the Base Exchange, we found ourselves within sight of the tankers, converted Boeing 707s, that refueled the Boeing-made bombers in midair. Being avid photographers, we took out our gear to shoot pictures. Before the cameras were up to our eyes an air policeman, who appeared out of nowhere, calmly ordered us to stop. If you were near the planes, you were being watched. You could not even take a photo of one support system for The Bomb.

Today, I speed down the main runway with not a guard in sight. As we hurtle down the flight line in a roadster with the top down, the driver tells me about the rock concert held on this tarmac. Phish, with their longhaired, happy-go-lucky fans, took the place of the deadly serious airmen and officers in their crew cuts. More proof the Cold War is over.

We head down a side road that leads from the runway and soon see double chain-link fences topped with razor wire. Behind these we see, partially buried, the bunkers that housed the bombs. Down another road we find the smaller bunkers that guarded the nuclear hearts of the weapons. Nature is reclaiming these old storehouses of death; grass and bushes poke through the concrete where military vehicles once carried the agents of Armageddon to and from the planes. The only signs of activity are the huge piles of dirt, which are contaminated with jet fuel and only-the-EPA-knows what else. A facility the size of this base was bound to produce some toxic results that required cleaning.

Seeing all of this immediately after walking around our former quarters in the housing area has blown new fire from the banked coals of memories. All of those feelings that I suppressed in my youth—fear of Dad dying in a plane crash, fear of my own death signaled by a blinding flash over the base, anxiety over my father's whole role in the end of the world, and all the gnawing uncertainty of that period—have now reignited and demand my attention.

We leave the base. No longer proclaiming "Peace is Our Profession," the sign now boasts of the base's new role as a commerce center; swords to plowshares and all that.

The Cold War is over, but just as the base needs some overdue cleaning, so do my emotions. Even with the knowledge, I possess a most satisfying grin for the rest of the day.

100 Years in the Allagash
By Cathie Pelletier

Grandfather, the day you were born, April 7, 1887, Jefferson Davis, the President of the Confederacy, gave a fiery speech in New Orleans. He was 79 years old, and *The New York Times* referred to him as Jeff. With this hundred years you have lived, with this long covered bridge spanning a century, you have linked your great-great-grandchildren to the past. Jeff Davis spoke on a balmy April afternoon in New Orleans, amid the cheers of a loyal crowd, and far away in northern Maine you were welcomed to the planet Earth. Jesse James had been dead for five years. Custer had already made his wild mistake at Little Big Horn, eleven years earlier, and so had Wild Bill Hickok, holding his famous poker hand in the Mann and Lewis Saloon, Dakota Territories, his back fatally to the door. These stories were the headlines your own father heard in his day. They are no more than legend to us now, but did he tell them to you while they were still fresh and alive?

I remember the toast of homemade bread you made on the top of the kitchen's wood stove, on those wintry mornings when the raw wind rolled in off the river. There was Grammie's cranberry sauce, molasses cake, and the pot of tea forever on the stove. I knew this breakfast waited in the kitchen on those blustery mornings, the linoleum carpet so cold to warm feet. Those mornings of the high snowbanks, Grampie, and the low temperatures, with school waiting on the other side of the one-way bridge. Those mornings when you came to the foot of the stairs to wake my cousin and me. "Little girls. It's time to get up." Wood snapped and popped in the kitchen stove while we ate our breakfast, and Grammie's French accent filled the big warm room like a soft litany brought over from the old country.

On April 7, 1887, the day you were born, *The New York Times* spoke of the women suffragettes fighting for their rights in Kansas. "The advent of the petticoat in politics," the paper warned, "where ladies hover among the men." It would be thirty-three more years before women would vote. Grover Cleveland was our president. Many vessels wrecked at sea in massive storms off the coasts of California and New England are now tragedies long forgotten. The latest rage in refrigerators was the Monroe Patent, with its glazed stoneware lining, and its guarantee not to "sweat, get musty, or sour." Fine fashion shoes with Spanish arches that promised to save female feet from the nuisance of tacks and small nails, were selling for the expensive price of $3.00 a pair. They are back in style now, Grandfather, these shoes. Today at the mall I saw young girls with their feet laced up tight and snug as their great-grandmothers'. Young girls, caught up in the excitement of life, who think their fancy shoes are new.

On April 7, 1887, the spring collars and cuffs went on sale for a dime each, and Easter scarfs were going for forty-four cents. I have bought these cuffs and collars at auctions, and I have wondered about the women and men of a hundred years ago who must have worn them. They are yellow with age. The cleaners tell me they will crumble if tampered with, so I keep them tucked safely away. But do you remember them, Grandfather, when they were white and starched and stylish?

I still see the ferryboats, and towboats, and bateaux you built, small replicas of the dinosaurs that once were a common sight on the rivers. I've seen you hold the models on your front lawn for visitors to admire. They were good as gold in your large hands. "I used to build the real boats in my prime," you tell them. Every book or magazine article written on the lumbering industry in northern Maine refers to you with respect and admiration. You were a friend to every passer-by.

I dream of you often, Grampie. We are back in your old home and we are looking for Grammie in the narrow rooms upstairs. We search the summer kitchen and the lilting front porch. We are forever looking. This is the dream of guilt. This is the dream the young still dare to dream. I stopped coming to visit you when you no longer knew who I was. On one of those last visits I saw you staring at a small picture on the wall of a beautiful Victorian woman in a fashionable pink dress, with a matching pink parasol. It was the kind of print department stores are famous for selling. I took it off the wall and put it in your hands. You rubbed one finger across the surface of the glass. "This was my mother," you said softly. "Her name was Mary Jane Hafford. She was a good woman." I know your memories are of her now, and your father, Nizaire, and somewhere, now, you are still crossing cars on your precious ferry, a task you did for thirty-three summers.

When you were ten years old the new 1897 Credenda bicycles were on sale for $18.50, a rich man's sum. It would be another six years before the Model A rolled into existence, and many more before you saw your first. I know, Grandfather, that when an automobile went past in those days, men dropped what they were doing to run across their planted fields, in hopes of just a glimpse of it. An *auto* mobile. A creature that ran all by itself. And women brought their children indoors for fear of them being run down by the slow-moving monster, barely able to achieve bicycle speed. Oh, Grandfather, what an incredible thing it must have been to see the automobile for the first time! Do you know that nowadays teenagers grumble if they don't own one?

What glories we miss these days. It doesn't surprise us that the Concorde zips from New York to London in two and a half hours.

Did you ever hear about the Concorde? Would you believe me if I told you, you who were sixteen when the Wright brothers managed to keep their little biplane off the ground over Kitty Hawk for 59 seconds?

When you were twenty-one, Postum bragged that it was free from harmful coffee poison and that it would "build up broken down brain and nerve cells and no one needs this more than the chronic coffee drinker." It would protect you from what doctors were calling "coffee heart." The advertisement railed against caffeine in harsher terms than we nowadays use to describe cocaine.

A few weeks before you married my French-speaking grandmother, Edith Thibodeau, the *Titanic* plowed against a mountain of ice and went to a watery grave off the coast of Newfoundland. It has resurfaced, Grandfather, this legendary ship, at least on our television screens. Your marriage produced eleven children. Nowadays you have forty-two grand-children, ninety-one great-grandchildren, and nine great-great grandchildren. Your grandchildren have branched out from the family tree and are spread around the world, a world you never visited, or cared to, really. You were content with your front porch, your rocking chair, those miniature boats, your stories of the log drives, and the familiar sound of the Allagash River meeting the St. John. I can still hear your large laugh, and the thunderous clap of your hands coming together at the end of a humorous story.

You experienced the pain of losing a son to war when Melford died aboard the USS *Wasp* in the South Pacific. A faceless pilot, his plane sporting the Rising Sun of Japan on the side, swooped in out of a morning's fog and dropped a 1,600-pound incendiary bomb. Remember the telegram, Grandfather, on that day so many years ago? *We regret to inform you* . . . War is all regret. I hope this is the lesson your great-great-grandchildren will carry with them to the future.

Your youngest child, Rochelle, did not outlive you. She died of cancer in 1985, but this was painful news you were spared. With two years still to live, you did not remember you had a child named

Rochelle. And I'm glad that you didn't know of the death of your beloved house, a proud house in its prime. There are hazelnut and chokecherry bushes growing where it stood. But your grandchildren, who knew it well and loved it, will pass its memory on to their children, and to their grandchildren. We will keep the house alive for you, Grampie. This is the least we can do.

When Grandmother died a part of you died, too. And it never came back. I saw you lingering at her grave, cane in hand for that bad knee, while the December winds whipped your coat about you. She had spent forty-two days in the hospital at Fort Kent, and you found forty-two different ways to get rides to town and have lunch with her. You sat by her bedside until visiting hours were over. Forty-two rides, which sometimes included the milkman. Forty-one nights my father, Louis, went down to see his mother and bring you home. What I remember most about Grammie's funeral was your pain. And that same night as you tried to fall asleep, knowing that your life's companion was gone, I was sixteen and studying for a college biology exam in the next bedroom. "Little girl," you said. I went in to talk to you and found you'd been crying. "I don't know what I'm gonna do without Mum. We've been all these years together." What could I say? "You'll be okay, Grampie," I said. "You still have many good years left."

Then I had to study for my biology exam. I think of the irony in this often now that I'm years away from it. There you were, involved in the greatest biological test of your lifetime. But it didn't go unnoticed, all of this, Grandfather. The elderly turn up in my fiction often, more than any other group, and they suffer some, yes, but they are brave. They are dignified. They are fighters for a vanishing generation of people. I owe you this.

When Neil Armstrong walked on the moon, I remember a ride down from your house with my father. The moon was a huge yellow wafer over the tops of the pines. You'd been watching it, thoughtfully.

"You'd think it would break," you said finally, "when they step on it."
You thought it was hollow, the glorious moon. Now, Grandfather, I
see the poetry in what you said. I understand this now, in the year of
the space shuttle. The truth is that the moon of your generation was
meant to light up the river, that blessed highway. It was there to turn
the granite tombstones of your ancestors into silver. The moon belonged
to the ragged pines, and the silent hulk of the ferryboat bobbing at the

shoreline. People had no business walking on the moon when there was still work to be done here on Earth, the garden planted, the hay cut, the logs sawed into lumber. Now I understand.

Here in your 100th year, Grandfather, a supernova was first spotted from northern Chile. Its light has been coming toward us for 170,000 years, traveling at 186,000 miles per second. This is the vastness of the universe we live in. Your offspring are like this starlight, moving down the years, reaching generation after generation. This is our testimony to you. Through us you will touch the face of the next century, and the one after that, and the one after that . . . if man is careful with his weapons. This is our legacy of fear nowadays, Grampie. Our generation has been so clever we have the power to destroy ourselves, like a huge star collapsing. But we will do our best. That's all you have ever asked of us.

Home
By Kent Ward

On a glorious blue-sky Aroostook County day in June of 1962 I set off to take a job as Rockland bureau chief for the *Bangor Daily News* after eight years as editor of my hometown weekly newspaper, the now-defunct *Limestone Leader*.

As I crossed The County line south of Sherman and sounded the obligatory farewell toot on my car horn, I vowed to return someday, although I knew it probably would not be until retirement well down the road. When I finally did return permanently in 2006 after selling my Winterport property where I had lived for three decades, I had been gone precisely forty-four years, three months and one day.

Despite author Tom Wolfe's admonition to the contrary, I've always felt that you can go home again, provided home is where the heart is. And I'm reminded with each memorable County sunrise that the daily rewards justify the long wait.

Ten years after I had retired from a nearly thirty-year career with the *BDN*, I purchased a run-down property with a great panoramic view on a high plateau three miles southwest of Limestone village, not far from the homestead where I was born and raised.

Most every weekend for the ensuing five-plus years I made the nearly 400-mile round trip from Winterport to renovate the home that once had served as a parsonage for a little crossroads country church that no longer stands.

From my one-acre allotment of Paradise, I can see forever, surrounded by fields of broccoli, potatoes and grain; shades of green and brown and gold in season under azure skies to make the heart sing and the pulse quicken.

The breeze, a near-constant companion, is Mother Nature's antidote to any potential black-fly problem. Thirty miles to the south, Mars Hill Mountain dominates the horizon, seemingly close enough to reach out and touch on days when the light is just so. To the east, the gentle hills of western New Brunswick lead the eye to rest on the queen of the range, Blue Bell Mountain. God was truly on his game when he laid out the panorama I behold daily, free of charge.

In most any direction I face, much of the fertile farmland slopes up to meet the sky in the distance, sans trees, buildings or other obstructions to break the mesmerizing impression that I am truly in Big Sky Country. Breathing space I have, in spades.

And quiet. Many years ago, when a young nephew from Philadelphia was visiting the family here in The County, he turned to his mother one night and said, "Mum, it's so quiet up here it hurts your ears."

After spending years listening to heavy truck traffic negotiating the hill outside my Winterport windows, gears a-grinding and engine brakes ca-chugging at all hours of the night, I understand perfectly what the lad meant. The sounds I hear these days are almost exclusively the reassuring daytime sounds of farm equipment working the land. The night belongs to the crickets, and perhaps the occasional hoot owl, until the crows and songbirds sound reveille at day's dawning.

I have come to realize that a major part of the pull of The County for me, and perhaps for other former expatriates as well, is space—wide open space, grand vistas and distant horizons that promote a permanently exhilarating feeling of not being fenced in. The freedom to move about without bumping into the furniture, so to speak, or not treading on someone else's trap line is a cherished gift.

It is the people, though, who make the place special. Although I have found residents of several areas of the state in which I have lived to be a generally laid-back and sociable lot, eager to lend a helping hand to a neighbor in time of need, County people take a back seat to no one in this regard.

I have had my driveway plowed by a stranger just passing by after a serious overnight snowstorm, no pay accepted, and have been offered freshly caught trout by another stranger who stopped by to chat while I was mowing my lawn. I have had a peck of prime Russet bakers left on my doorstep by a nearby farmer's gregarious hired man. And I have been good-naturedly ribbed that, because I took my sweet old time coming back to The County, I am now officially considered to be "from away"—if not a man without a country, then one who is on probation until I can re-establish my County bona fides.

One day last fall as I drove into town I encountered two local potato farmers in their potato trucks, one headed north, the other headed south, blocking the highway while they talked things over for a spell. I knew that they were not about to move out of the way until the conversation had run its course, and that honking my pickup's horn in the interest of nudging them along would be a mistake only a tourist might make, though likely only once.

And so I sat there smiling at the realization that it had been forty-four years since I had last experienced this particular trademark County ritual. In a fast-changing world, some things simply never change. I was back home. And I had passed my first re-entry test.

Contributors

Dorothy Anderson ("New Sweden Athletes") lives in Thetford, Vermont, with her husband, Richard Balagur, where she retired as Associate Dean at Granite State College in New Hampshire. A New Sweden native with graduate degrees in environmental education and community development from the University of Maine, she wrote "New Sweden Athletes" for her father, Edmund Anderson, who skied from the time he could walk until his nineties and who helped found the New Sweden Athletic Club.

Jeanette Baldridge ("Mysteries of March in Maine") is a freelance writer with roots in New Mexico. She has taught at the University of Maine and for Adult Education in Bethel, Maine, and is the former editor and publisher of *Out of the Cradle* literary journal. She and her husband, Don, now operate LolliePapa Farm in West Paris.

The Rev. Barry Blackstone ("Clearing the Land") grew up on a potato farm in Perham and served eight years as pastor of the Calvary Baptist Church in Westfield. He now lives in Ellsworth where he is pastor of the Emmanuel Baptist Church.

Frank Bolton ("The White Pine") and his wife, Houlton native Barbara McGillicuddy Bolton, live in Brooklyn, New York, and summer on East Grand Lake in Orient, Maine.

Kristine Bull Bondeson ("The Scandinavian Way") gardens, knits, reads, writes occasionally, and bakes in Woodland.

Davis Chung ("Clean-up") is a 1978 graduate of Caribou High School who earned a degree in history from the University of Southern Maine.

Lately, he creates publications and graphics for an aviation consulting company and lives in North Carolina.

The late **Cherry Bolstridge Danker** ("Finding the Cedar Spring") retired to her hometown of Portage in 1986 after a thirty-four-year career with the Veterans' Administration in Washington, D.C. She lived at the edge of Portage Lake and became active in writers' groups, happy to pursue creative writing instead of "federal gobbledegook."

John Dombek ("Sweet Corn," "Horses") grew up in Houlton, where his exploits with his twin brother, Joe, provided fodder for a collection of stories titled *Joe and Me*. His career in commercial writing, advertising and marketing eventually took him to Santa Clara, Utah, where he lives with his wife, Barbara, and has published a novel and several children's books.

Linda R. Emery ("Harvest 1961") grew up in Caribou, and became a registered nurse specializing in critical care and emergency medicine. She is fiercely proud of her Aroostook County roots and credits her times in the potato fields with a strong lifelong work ethic. Now retired, she continues to enjoy writing and lives in Cumberland Center, with her husband, Brian.

Dan Ennis, aka Medicine Voice, ("My First Day of School") was born at the Tobique Indian Reservation in New Brunswick, grew up in Caribou, and returned to his home where he honors his ancestors by keeping their traditions and stories alive through writing and community activities.

The late **Gordon Espling**, ("The Last of the First") a native of Caribou, earned accounting degrees from Husson University and Embry-Riddle Aeronautical University and served as a finance officer at Fort Drum,

New York, and the New England Corps of Engineers in Waltham, Massachusetts. Retired from the U.S. Army Reserves in 1988, he divided his time between homes in Boynton Beach, Florida, and Eagle Lake, and taught accounting for Jefferson Community College in Watertown, New York, Husson College and the University of Maine at Fort Kent.

The late **Gordon Hammond** (pen-and-ink drawings and "The Wellspring") moved to Westfield in the 1970s following a career in advertising and graphic design in New York and Boston. A native of Long Island, New York, he was dedicated to sustainable living and used his creative talents to celebrate Aroostook County until his death in 2016. Co-founder of *Echoes* magazine, he was a prolific artist and writer, producing two novels, *The Orphan* and *The Family*, two collections of stories, *Leaving Home* and *Lisa's Dream*, and countless illustrations for *Echoes*.

The late **Gwen Haley Harmon** ("Henderson School," "A Horse with an Attitude") grew up on a potato farm in Woodland, nine miles from Caribou, descended from Irish immigrants who left Ireland to escape famine. She published her stories in a collection titled *This I Remember* so future generations would better understand their origins. She worked in Caribou elementary schools thirty-five years—twenty-two as a teacher and thirteen as a supervisor.

The late **Elizabeth Rundlett Pray Hull** ("A Night at the Vaughan House") was a New Hampshire native and graduate of Fryeburg Academy whose great-uncle, Owen E. Blackden, was the source of her stories. **Jane Beckwith,** her daughter and transcriber of tales, lives in Cape Elizabeth, with her husband, Gary, a native of Mapleton.

Leonard and the late **Phyllis Schwartz Hutchins** ("Our Winter Playground") grew up in Fort Fairfield and operated Oxbow Lodge in

Oxbow for eighteen years. He earned bachelor's and master's degrees from the University of Maine in Orono, served in the military, taught school in Hampden and Ashland and spent summers working for the Maine Forest Service. His publications include a novel, *Bon Homme*, and collections of stories: *Gram, Is He Telling me the Truth?* and *Legends and Lore*. **Sister Mary Denis** (Alene Schwartz, Phyllis' sister) was an elementary school teacher and administrator with the Sisters of Mercy in Portland for sixty years and served a double term as Mother Superior.

The late **Dorothy Boone Kidney** ("Saturday Night on Main Street," "What Depression?," "Rubbing Elbows") grew up in Presque Isle and taught school in Yarmouth, Gray and Washburn. She and her husband, Milford, spent twenty-eight summers in a one-room cabin in the Allagash, providing her with material for three books. She also wrote children's and inspirational books and articles for national and regional magazines.

Ron Laing ("Stranded on a School Bus," "Good Neighbors," "The Barrel Man") pursues writing and photography in Oxford. A native of Westfield, he graduated from Presque Isle High School and married his high school sweetheart, Carolyn Dudley. They lived in Massachusetts for forty-five years and raised two daughters. He is the author of *An African Adventure, Egypt Road* and *From Country Roads to City Streets*.

The late **Linwood Lawrence** ("Night Flight"), a 1934 graduate of Houlton High School, spent fifty years flying and maintaining airplanes, including fifteen years at the Houlton airport. In retirement, he built three airplanes in Palm City, Florida, all of which are still flying—one in Utah, one in Texas, and one in Maine.

The late **Paul Lucey** ("Heroes of 1947") was a retired high school social science teacher and administrator. A graduate of Brown University, he served in World War II and the Korean conflict as a U. S. Marine Corps fighter and helicopter pilot. The late **Fran Robinson Mitchell** was a native of Stacyville Plantation and graduate of Ricker Classical Institute in Houlton. She attended the University of Maine in Orono until World War II led her to enlist in the U.S. Marine Corps, where she graduated from Motor Transport School at Camp Lejeune, North Carolina.

Sandy Lynch ("Friendly Village") and her husband, Jerry, were married in 1972 at the United States Merchant Marine Academy in Kings Point, Long Island, New York, where they met. They live in Trumbull, Connecticut, and are the parents of a son and two daughters.

Writer/Photographer **Darrell McBreairty** ("The St. John River Valley"), a native of Allagash, graduated from the University of Maine at Fort Kent and New York Institute of Photography. *Alcatraz Eel: The John Stadig Files* and *Allagash Summers: The Philip Calvin Hughey Sr. Photographs* are available from the author at dmcbreairty@yahoo.com.

Brook Merrow (Cover image photographer), a native of Kennebunk Beach, now lives in Bozeman, Montana, with her husband, Hy Adelman. They have two sons, who also live in Bozeman. She was an early contributor to *Echoes* when her husband was farming with his father, Milton Adelman, in Mars Hill.

Amy Morin ("A Farmer's Wife") worked at the University of Maine in Orono for twenty-seven years, nine in forestry and eighteen at the Canadian-American Center. She lives in Old Town where she has worked with the French Island project *Nos Histoires de l'Île* (Our stories of the island). The group interviewed 39 people who grew up on French Island in the early to mid-1900s and produced a book of the history of the island with stories from the interviews. In her retirement, Amy gives presentations about this project to classes at the university.

Bobbie Morrow ("Le Grand Ménage") resides in Presque Isle and enjoys keeping in touch with the people and places of the beautiful St. John Valley where she was born and raised.

Cathie Pelletier ("Haying," "100 Years in the Allagash") is a novelist and screenwriter who has returned to Allagash and the family homestead where she was born. Her career was launched with a trilogy of novels set in a town called Mattagash. Fifteen books later, her work has been translated into many languages and two novels were adapted for television. Currently writing nonfiction, her last book was *Proving Einstein Right*, co-authored with S. James Gates, a National Medal of Science winner.

Jenny Radsma ("Crossing the Border," "Secret Pleasure") moved south from northwestern Alberta in the 1990s to live in the St. John Valley where she has taught nursing at the University of Maine at Fort Kent for more than twenty years. When she's not writing she's biking, hiking, skiing, traveling, cooking, and sometimes napping.

Lana Robinson ("Spring Peepers"), a native of Sherman, earned bachelor's and master's degrees from the University of Maine in Orono and taught at Katahdin Junior and Senior high schools in Sherman Station for more than thirty years.

Candide and the late **Harold Sedlick** ("The Old Pump") traveled every summer from their home in Connecticut to their 200-acre farm in Madawaska, which had been in her family for generations. A retired tool engineer, Harold's experiences on the farm inspired him to write about life in rural Maine.

The late **Margaret Mueller Shore** ("The Pay-off for Picking") was a native of Madawaska and a retired professor of biomedical sciences at the University of Maine at Augusta. With a doctorate in health policy, she worked at the Maine Center for Disease Control and Prevention directing a program to reduce healthcare-associated infections in Maine hospitals and nursing homes.

The late **Glenna Johnson Smith** ("Tell Me the Landscape," "Winter Shoes," "Rural Aroostook Women," "Learning Together") grew up in Ashville, Maine, and moved to Aroostook County as a bride in 1941. A graduate of the University of Maine in Orono, she taught English at Presque Isle High School, wrote and directed plays and served as poetry editor for *Echoes* magazine, for which she wrote the column Old County Woman for twenty-five years. She also has two books, *Old Maine Woman* and *Return of Old Maine Woman,* published by Islandport Press.

Jane Russell Stanford ("Helping Hands," "Under One Roof," "Countin' Tickets") grew up on a potato farm in Fort Fairfield, and now lives in Bangor where she hosts a blog: janestanford.blogspot.com.

A native of Houlton, **Torrey Sylvester** ("My Father's Pine Boxes") lived in his beloved Aroostook County for most of his life and only recently moved to southern Maine with his wife, Jennifer, to be nearer their children and grandchildren.

Pamela Stoddard Taylor ("Thirty Cents a Barrel") grew up in Presque Isle and graduated from Presque Isle High School in 1974. She lives in Farmington where she taught fourth- and-fifth graders until her retirement.

The late **Merle Tyrrell** ("The Year with No Summer") was born in Houlton and graduated from Houlton High School. He worked for the Almon H. Fogg Company until 1990, traveling to every town, city, hamlet and village in Aroostook County.

Kent Ward ("Home") is a retired associate managing editor of the *Bangor Daily News* where his weekend op-ed page column earned him the title "The Old Dawg." The Limestone native was inducted into the Maine Press Association Hall of Fame in 2004.

Mary Warren ("The Moose in my Backyard") grew up in Old Town, and lived in New York City and the Philadelphia area before returning to live in Aroostook County in 2005. A guidance counselor at Presque Isle High School, she now lives in Fort Fairfield.

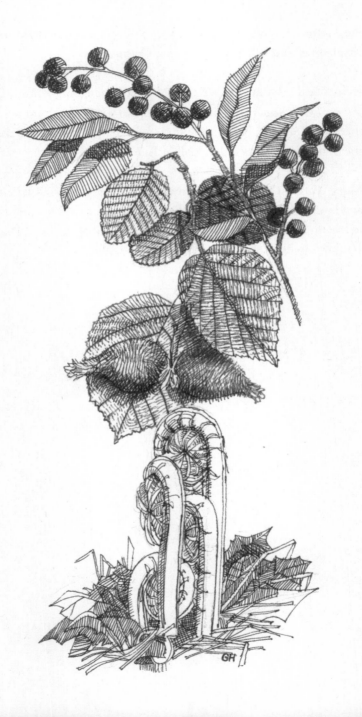

Acknowledgments

Sincere thanks to the following people for their valuable contributions to this anthology: Shannon Butler for planting the seed, Dean Lunt for making it grow, Taylor McCafferty for always responding to questions, Kristine Bondeson and Jenny Radsma for proofreading, Christina Kane-Gibson for cheerleading, the team of readers who helped select the stories (Kristine Bondeson, Cindy Edgecomb and Ken Hixon) and all the writers (or their heirs) who so graciously gave permission for republication of their stories.

About the Editor

Kathryn Olmstead is a former *Bangor Daily News* columnist and editor/publisher of *Echoes* magazine, based in Caribou, Maine, which she co-founded in 1988. She served twenty-five years on the journalism faculty of the University of Maine in Orono, the last six as associate dean in the College of Liberal Arts and Sciences. Her writing has appeared in the *Christian Science Monitor, USA Today, The World and I, American Journalism Review, Maine Townsman,* and *Islandport Magazine.* She also co-authored a World War II memoir *Flight to Freedom: World War II Through the Eyes of a Child* with Bangor portrait photographer Philomena Baker published in 2013. She founded the Maine Center for Student Journalism in 1993 and was inducted into the Maine Press Association Hall of Fame in 2018. Before joining the UMaine faculty, she was a correspondent for the *Bangor Daily News,* editor of the *Aroostook Republican* weekly newspaper in Caribou, agricultural columnist for regional and national newspapers in Vermont and Kansas, and district representative for U.S. Sen. Bill Cohen. A native of Battle Creek, Michigan, she earned a bachelor of arts in English from the University of Illinois, Champaign-Urbana, and a master of arts in English and education from the University of Wisconsin, Madison. She taught English and journalism in Wisconsin and New Hampshire before moving to Maine in 1974.